OPERATION CHARIOT
The Raid on St. Nazaire

COMMANDOS
OPERATION CHARIOT
The Raid on St Nazaire

JON COOKSEY

with contributions from:

James G. Dorrian • Robin Neillands

Pen & Sword
MILITARY

First published in Great Britain in 2005 by
Pen & Sword Military an imprint of
Pen & Sword Books Ltd
47 Church Street
Barnsley
South Yorkshire
S70 2AS

ISBN 1-84415-116-6

A CIP catalogue record for this book is
available from the British Library

Printed and bound in Singapore by
Kyodo Printing Co (Singapore) Pte Ltd

For a complete list of Pen & Sword titles please contact
PEN & SWORD BOOKS LIMITED
47 Church Street, Barnsley, South Yorkshire, S70 2AS, England
E-mail: enquiries@pen-and-sword.co.uk
Website: www.pen-and-sword.co.uk

CONTENTS

ACKNOWLEDGEMENTS

I owe a great debt of gratitude to the contributors who have all given the project their wholehearted support. I have been very fortunate indeed to enlist both Rob Neillands and Jim Dorrian to the cause. As an ex-Royal Marine and respected military historian and author, Rob Neillands' credentials are impeccable and his contribution on the development of the concept of 'raiding' opens the book in fine style. His piece is followed almost seamlessly by Jim Dorrian's contribution on the planning process behind Operation Chariot. There can be few people who can match Jim's depth of knowledge on the raid or the personalities who took part. He has been a welcome source of encouragement and has checked several sections for errors. If any remain, then they are entirely due to oversights on my part.

Thanks are also due to Dr. David Paton who, as a Captain in the RAMC and a member of No. 2 Commando sailed into St. Nazaire aboard ML 307. He kindly made available his unpublished account of his experiences of the raid, extracts of which appear in the book. Other extracts from the oral testimonies of Sir Ronald Swayne, Mr. Ralph Batteson and Mr. Harold Roberts, all of whom took part in the raid, are from the Sound Archive of the Imperial War Museum and are reproduced with the kind permission of the Trustees. I am indebted to John Stopford-Pickering, Peter Hart and Richard Hughes of the Sound Archive for their unfailing courtesy, good humour and patience during my visits or when responding to my communications.

Once again Jon Wilkinson's eye for detail in just the right place has brought the text to life. His patience in responding to and then actually realising some of my more 'extreme' ideas is a source of constant amazement. Thank you Jon.

Finally, my wife Heather and daughter Georgia have, once again, been a constant source of support and encouragement. I couldn't do it without them.

Jon Cooksey

Reading 2004

INTRODUCTION

Commandos. The word has captured the imagination and inspired awe and fear in equal measure down the decades since World War Two. It conjures up images of hard, fearless men with blackened faces – their fighting skills honed to a razor sharp edge of combat perfection – striking silently and swiftly at the very heart of the enemy. It conveys secrecy, ruthlessness, danger and sacrifice, and, although they weren't officially 'Commandos', in the dark and desperate days of the summer of 1940, the actions of these men brought hope to the British people.

Amongst the first to bring such hope were a party of 120 officers and men of a strange, new unit called Number 11 Independent Company, led by Major Ronnie Tod. On the morning of June 25th Britons woke to the amazing news that the previous night Tod's force had crossed the English Channel, landed between Boulogne and Etaples and inflicted casualties on German troops, before returning home without loss. The news of the raid, code-named Collar, was seized eagerly by a nation frantic to feed on any crumbs of success that might otherwise supplement the diet of 'cold comfort' offered by the 'miracle' of Dunkirk. By late June 1940, Britain needed every crumb of comfort she could muster, for Britain now stood alone and in mortal danger.

The outlook was bleak. Surely it was only a matter of time before the Germans descended on an almost defenceless Britain to pound her into submission? And yet, amidst all these 'black' events, Operation Collar offered the faintest of glimmers, the most slender shaft of light to pierce the gloom. In spite of a lack of resources and Germany's total domination of Europe, Britain had shown that she would fight on, indeed, had shown that she could fight on. Britain had reached beyond her shores to carry the war to occupied Europe.

Keen to wrest back the initiative from Germany, Churchill had already made clear his views on Britain adopting such a policy. Operation Collar was a very small and, as it turned out, not very well planned enterprise and although such 'pin prick' raids earned Churchill's scorn, the concept of continued raiding was nevertheless established. There were no illusions that such raids would bring about the imminent demise of Nazi Germany but little by little, the raids ensured that Germany began to commit an inordinate amount of men, material and time to the defence of its lengthy occupied coastline in northern Europe. At home the morale boosting benefits were vastly out of proportion to the actual damage inflicted on the Germans in France, but it sent a clear signal to those abroad who might look favourably on Britain's cause that if she was to go down, then she would go down fighting. Thus had the Commandos been born.

A year later and the Combined Operations Directorate, an organisation set up specifically to co-ordinate necessarily joint-Service operations, was well and truly established with a steady stream of plans flowing in for consideration.

In late June 1941 a meeting of the Executive Planning Staff, chaired by Captain G.A. French, convened to consider possible 'runners' from the scores of raiding schemes already submitted. Winnowing out the more offbeat, over-complex or downright foolhardy, the meeting settled on Operation Chess – a proposal for a reconnaissance raid - as its first choice. Two further operations – Acid Drop and Chopper – were pencilled in for August and September. During a lull in the formal deliberations, Lieutenant Commander G. Gonin, the representative of the Naval Intelligence Department, mentioned to Captain French an idea, prompted by the sinking of the 40,000-ton German battleship *Bismarck* a month earlier, that he and his colleagues had been considering. The *Bismarck* – damaged by an air-launched torpedo and leaking fuel after her encounter with the British ships HMS *Hood* and *Prince of Wales*, had been making for the vast *Normandie* dock at St. Nazaire - the only dry dock on the French Atlantic coast capable of accommodating her mighty frame - when the British finally snared and sank her on 27th May. The *Bismarck* was no longer a threat but her sister ship, the equally mighty *Tirpitz*, was still at large and the great fear was that she could pay a visit to St. Nazaire and the *Normandie* dock at any day, with all the attendant menace to Allied shipping that such a move might bring.

French listened with interest as Gonin outlined an embryonic scheme for the destruction of the *Normandie* dock. It was to prove a seminal moment in the history of Combined Operations raiding. Referred for consideration, the germ of the idea was committed to paper for the first time in the diary of Sir Roger Keyes, the then Director of Combined Operations, later in July under its codename - Chariot.

Thus conceived, the plan was to endure a troubled gestation before its final realisation.

A first attempt at hatching a plot to hit St. Nazaire came on 10th August 1941 when the Admiralty charged Sir Charles Forbes, then Commander-in-Chief Plymouth, to liase with Combined Operations in coming up with a suitable scheme. Two objectives had been identified: the destruction or disabling of the lock gates and an attack on U-Boat pens. Forbes weighed up the pros and cons and submitted a detailed appreciation in which he highlighted the risks of detection of a large force on a long and perilous sea voyage; the lack of suitable craft to carry enough fuel for a return trip; the dangers of the shoals and shallow waters on the approach up the Loire estuary and the sheer magnitude of the task of achieving that most favoured of weapons for raiders – surprise – by sailing a tortuous six miles up a major river whose banks bristled with German guns. Another review and a meeting at the Admiralty on 19th September saw the plan trip over similar stumbling blocks. Keyes's representative at that meeting had by now indicated that the Commando landing force necessary to carry out such a job would be near the 300 mark, excluding the demolition parties. That would be some raid.

Turned down once again in late October 1941 - just days after Mountbatten took over the reins of Combined Operations from Sir Roger Keyes on the 27th - detailed planning for Chariot did not get under way until three months later. The spark this time had come from Churchill himself who, on 26th January 1942, had raised the issue of destroying the *Normandie* dock again during a meeting with Admiral of the Fleet Sir Dudley Pound. The next day the Admiralty asked Mountbatten to look afresh at the implications of mounting an operation against St. Nazaire and he, in turn, handed the problem to his team of Intelligence and Planning 'Advisers' at Combined Operations HQ (COHQ). The die was cast. By any stretch of the imagination Operation Chariot was to be the most ambitious, and dangerous raid yet staged; an audacious plan to mount a large-scale Commando raid on the *Normandie* dock using a loaned U.S. destroyer packed with high explosive as a battering ram. Offered odds on its success, even the most enthusiastic gambler might have been tempted to keep his money in his wallet but nevertheless a final version of the plan was approved on 3rd March 1942. Twenty-three days later the Chariot force set out on what history has recorded as the 'Greatest Raid of All' and for the Germans defending St. Nazaire the Allied 'invasion' came much earlier than they could ever have anticipated.

ST NAZAIRE
OPERATION CHARIOT

'THERE'S CERTAINLY A VC IN THIS' ON RAIDING

By Robin Neillands

Author and broadcaster Robin Neillands is a former Royal Marines Commando. He has written more than forty books on military history, including *The Raiders – The Army Commandos 1940-46* **(Weidenfeld and Nicolson 1989). A member of the British Commission for Military History, he lectures extensively and conducts battlefield tours in Europe and the United States.**

Historians of irregular warfare have come to call the St. Nazaire Raid – Operation CHARIOT – the greatest raid of all. This assessment is probably true – in daring, in skill of execution, in gallantry against odds and, above all, in results, the St. Nazaire Raid stands well beyond all the other Commando raids of the Second World War.

The raid also stands out because it comes almost at the end of the raiding phase for Britain's Commando forces. The Dieppe Raid, which took place a few months later, in August 1942, marks the start of a new phase - full-scale amphibious operations - for it involved an entire division of Canadian soldiers, warships and

aircraft as well as No. 3 and No. 4 Commandos and the Royal Marine 'A' Commando. The Dieppe Raid marked a change from raiding tasks carried out by a few men, perhaps a platoon, at most a company, to amphibious operations that were in fact preparations for the biggest amphibious operation of all, Operation Overlord, on D-Day, 6th June, 1944.

And yet the divide is not complete and the split not definitive; small scale raiding led to larger raids – like St. Nazaire – and so on to the big amphibious operations without which the enemy could not have been defeated; the Channel that protected Britain in 1940 was a moat that the Allied invasion armies had to cross in 1944.

Britain's Commando forces were formed in 1940, after the Dunkirk debacle, and for several very good reasons. First of all, in that dark hour, it was necessary to show the enemy, in spite of Dunkirk, that the spirit of resistance was still high among the British, that they would hit back at every opportunity and would carry the war to the enemy by whatever means were available, however small.

Nor was there long to wait. The French surrendered to the Germans on June 25th 1940. The first British unit to go by the name 'Commando'– John Durnford Slater's No. 3 Commando - was formed on June 28th and mounted its first raid, Operation Ambassador, on Guernsey just two weeks later, on the night of July 14th. For the next four years the Commandos were constantly in action, all over the world, from the snows of Norway to the jungles of South-East Asia, from the islands of the Adriatic to the beaches of Normandy - as the quote from the Second Book of Samuel says on the Commando memorial in Westminster Abbey – 'They performed whatsoever the King commanded.'

'They performed whatsoever the King commanded.'

The development of raiding forces by the British Army seems somewhat surprising for the British military mind tends to be conservative. The development of Commando forces was not welcomed with great enthusiasm at the War Office or among many parts of the Regular Army who regarded Commando soldiering as a diversion from the main task of defeating the enemy in the field by conventional means. The fact remains that during the Second World War no nation, or Army, did more to develop and foster the use of irregular forces than the British.

Irregular forces appeared in every theatre where the British Army was engaged – Chindits in the Far East and Burma, the Long Range Desert Group (LRDG) and the Special Air Service (SAS) in North Africa – where highly irregular units like the quaintly named Popski's Private Army – a force raiding in jeeps and commanded by a Polish émigré - was also born before going on to fight in Italy. To these can be added such little-known units as the Small Scale Raiding Force, which operated across the Channel in a fast motor boat engagingly entitled 'The Little Pisser', and the Royal Marine raiders of the Boom Patrol Detachment, the forerunner of the Special Boat Squadron or SBS, or COPP, the Combined Operations Pilotage Parties, that swam ashore by night to recce enemy beaches.

Nor was it just the Army and the Royal Marines – a Corps which produced nine Commando units during the Second World War and retains the Commando tradition to this day in the 3rd Commando Brigade, Royal Marines.

From the Royal Navy came the men of the Chariots, the human torpedoes, or those who served as frogmen or in midget submarines. From the RAF came the Mosquito squadrons of 2 Group, RAF, the air force aid for the French Maquis and other Resistance fighters in Occupied Europe, who raided the Gestapo H.Q. in Copenhagen, destroyed a U-boat commander's retreat in Brittany and released scores of condemned Frenchmen from the Gestapo prison at Amiens. Wherever there was an opportunity to smite the enemy, by land, sea or air the British created a force for that purpose. and some of these – the SAS, the SBS, the Commandos and the Parachute Regiment, survived the war and still form part of Britain's military organization

As it turned out Durnford Slater's Guernsey raid was a shambles – the landing craft were noisy, the men wore steel-shod boots, no Germans were found and when the time came to leave it was discovered that four men could not swim – the landing craft had been obliged to wait offshore - and had to be left behind. Prime Minister Winston Churchill described this operation as, 'a silly fiasco', adding that 'the idea of working up these coasts against us by pin-prick raids and fulsome communiqués is one to be strictly avoided'.

Prime Minister Winston Churchill. His interest in irregular raiding, prompted him to reconstruct, name and give vital support to the Commandos.

The Commandos needed and enjoyed Churchill's support, largely because he was always interested in irregular operations and in hitting back at the enemy. Churchill issued orders for the formation of raiding units even as Operation Dynamo – the Dunkirk evacuation was coming to an end in early June 1940. On June 4th he sent an instruction to the Chiefs of Staff stating that ' we should immediately set to work to organize small, self contained, thoroughly equipped raiding units'. On June 6th he sent another directive, stating that,

> 'Enterprises must be prepared with specially trained troops of the hunter class who can develop a reign of terror down the enemy coast.'

Apart from their creation, the Commando forces owed another debt to Winston Churchill – he gave them their name. When they were first created, the Commando units were officially known as 'Special Service Battalions', but the initials SS, with its Nazi connotations, did not go down well with the units; Lieutenant Colonel Durnford-Slater would reply to any communication addressed to 'No. 3 SS Battalion' by signing himself as 'CO, No. 3 Commando'.

The SS dagger badge of the Special Service Battalions. The SS initials were not popular with the units.

Churchill understood the objection and decreed that these raiding units should be known as 'Commandos', recalling that he, himself, had

11

Boer Commando units such as these, impressed Churchill with their professionalism and determined attacks on British troops occupying South Africa.

Churchill being paraded in front of Boer spectators after his capture by the Commandos during the Boer War.

been captured by a Boer Commando unit during the South African War of 1899 –1902, during which mounted Commando units of rifle-armed burghers and farmers had held off the British Army for years. This distant war forged a later connection for in 1944 a number of South African officers were to serve with Commando units at Walcheren and during the advance to the Rhine. So the Commando units came to be formed and their exploits began to appear in the newspapers

Newspaper communiqués were another side-benefit of these early Commando operations. Headlines declaring that 'British Commandos raid French coast', were good for public morale and showed the public, in the USA as well as in Britain, that all was not lost; that the Army was ready to take the offensive.

The next benefit, and an on-going one, was that these raiding operations made the Powers-That-Be in Whitehall, the staff at Combined Operations Headquarters (COHQ), and the Commando colonels fully aware of what amphibious operations entailed. The mistakes of Guernsey were not repeated; the commanders learned that the men should be able to swim, that silent craft – and silent boots – were needed, that Commando operations needed intelligence information, careful planning and tight control.

Not least of these lessons lay in the need for specialised amphibious craft for the forthcoming invasion of Europe. When the Second World War began, the Royal Navy, then the largest Navy in the world, had exactly six landing craft; the best of these had a top speed of five knots and drew four feet of water.

On D-Day, 1944, the Allied invasion fleet, mustered off Normandy, contained some 6,000 landing craft of various sizes and types from the ocean going LST's (Landing Ship, Tank) down to the lowly LCA (Landing Craft, Assault) which could carry an infantry platoon. In between were LSI's (Landing Ship, Infantry), LCT's (Landing Craft, Tank) and a whole range of support craft, firing rockets or anti-

Commandos disembarking from a Landing Craft during an amphibious training excerise in Scotland.

aircraft guns to help the troops get ashore. The development of these craft, the need to develop and build an amphibious fleet, owes a great deal to the lessons learned in the early Commando raids and operations.

Other equipment was also developed; the Regular Army ammunition boot, comfortable but studded with nails, was replaced by the rubber or rope - soled SV boot, ideal for moving about quietly. The usual webbing equipment pack was replaced by the framed Bergen rucksack, into which enough stores for several days could be packed and carried.

With the development of kit went the development of tactics; Commandos learned to avoid the obvious landing spots and go ashore on rocky headlands or over difficult terrain, where their arrival would be unexpected - and developed cliff assault techniques to get up those cliffs in tactical formation.

With the development of new equipment and techniques went the rediscovery of old virtues. In the early days it had been thought that Commando soldiering would provide the maximum of action and excitement and the minimum of

A Commando was trained to avoid obvious landing spots and use difficult and rocky headlands to come ashore. This often resulted in climbing dangerous cliff faces in tactical formation.

bull. This prospect attracted many men who were temperamentally unsuited to irregular warfare, men who were resistant to discipline and reluctant to train. Their error was compounded by the understandable reluctance of Regular battalion COs to surrender their best men to the Commando recruiting teams, often using their arrival as a chance to rid the battalion of the incorrigible rogue, or the sick, lame and lazy.

The Commando colonels soon grew wise to this tactic and any men so provided were quickly RTU'd (Returned to Unit) as unsuitable – and the R.T.U. remained the Commando sanction for the rest of the war; if a man did not measure-up to the required standard there was no guardroom punishment; he was simply told to pack his bags and 'RTU'd. Slowly, but with increasing speed, the Commandos learned that a good unconventional soldier had to be a good conventional soldier first; fit, well-disciplined, good at weapon handling and field craft, self-reliant; a unit composed of such men would be a formidable force.

The idea that Commando soldiering provided an outlet for the wilder spirits, men attracted by the idea of crawling about at night with a blackened face and a knife between the teeth, was prevalent at the time and has proved hard to eradicate. The reality was very different; Commando soldiering was hard and relentless with few comforts and plenty of training, but hardship is the school of the soldier. Hard training weeded out the misfits and created a bond between those that endured it that would prove vital in battle and bind the Commando soldiers together for life.

Until 1942, the Commando units selected and trained their own men, the CO's showing considerable ingenuity in devising schemes to keep the men fit and interested. By 1942 however, it was considered necessary to standardise the training to some degree and to set up a system that could provide Commando units with a steady supply of trained and suitable soldiers. The solution was to set up a

Below left and right: Commando recruits had to undergo various stages of rigourous training in order to qualify as an accepted member the unit. Live ammunition was used and the recruits were allowed very few comforts.

Commando Basic Training Centre at Achnacarry, the home of a Highland chieftain, the Cameron of Locheil, near Fort William in the Scottish Highlands.

The six-week Commando course at Achnacarry soon acquired an awesome reputation for the gruelling nature of the training as one US Ranger, Bob Sales of the 29th Ranger Battalion explains:

Recruits undergoing an amphibious training exercise at the Commando Basic Training Centre, Achnacarry, Scotland.

'The 29th Division decided to form a Ranger battalion and I volunteered. We were interviewed and cross-examined as to why we wanted to do this and those who got through that went to this British Commando school, the toughest battle school in the world, up there in Scotland. The instructors were all experienced men who had been on raids to France. All the training used live ammunition and it went on day and night, no Sundays off with plenty of speed marching and cross country movement, all with full pack and loaded weapons. The training was hard and we were on British rations, which was like starving to death, but if you dropped out, you washed out and were out the gate. I was young and fit and very eager so I did pretty well and when the course was over we got a three-day pass to London where a young man simply had to have a good time.'

Bob Sales landed on Omaha beach on D-Day; everyone else on his boat was machine-gunned in the water and killed.

Training in unarmed combat gave the Commandos fighting confidence which augmented their aggression on raiding operations.

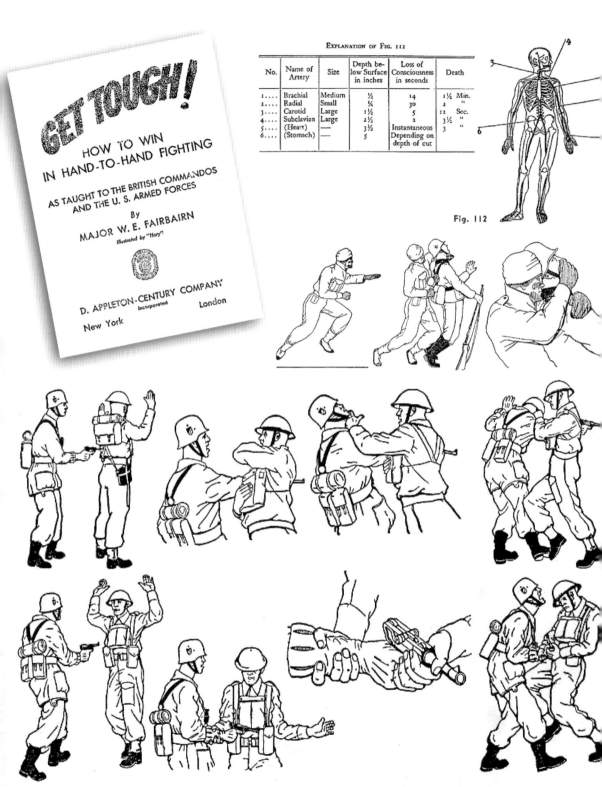

No.	Name of Artery	Size	Depth below Surface in inches	Loss of Consciousness in seconds	Death
1....	Brachial	Medium	½	14	1½ Min.
2....	Radial	Small	¼	30	2 "
3....	Carotid	Large	1½	5	12 Sec.
4....	Subclavian	Large	2½	2	3½ "
5....	(Heart)	—	3½	Instantaneous	3 "
6....	(Stomach)	—	5	Depending on depth of cut	

Fig. 112

Extracts from a booklet issued to British Commandos and US Forces. Written by Major Fairbairn, co-designer of the famous Commando fighting knife, it instructed elite units in the art of hand-to-hand fighting.

16

'UP HILL AND DOWN DALE'
COMMANDO TRAINING

By Harold Roberts. Ex – Lance Corporal, 2nd Battalion Liverpool Scottish and 5 Troop, No.2 Commando.

In 1940 I joined the Independent Companies. A few of us volunteered, we wanted to have a bash at this because we wanted to go and fight. Ours was No. 4 Independent Company based at Glenfinnan – the back of beyond. We were training – up hill and down dale - using live ammunition and explosives. We used to practise blowing up trees. We got used to handling explosives – guncotton and primers and such.

Number No. 2 Commando was formed at Paignton, from No. 4 Independent Company and the London Brigade because the London Scottish had a contingent just as the Liverpool Scottish had a contingent. I was in No. 5 Troop.

We used to do what we called speed marches. You used to have to carry all the weapons belonging to the Troop, disembowel the Bren Gun and instead of carrying the whole thing you used to carry parts – all the parts were divided up. Then you had to go on a speed march - so many miles in an hour- and we used to do seven or eight miles. Run hell for leather then jog, then walk and then you're off again. It was like a marathon. You got used to it. You had the fit, you had the super fit and then you had the hangers-on. The hangers on we stripped down and we carried their ammunition for them but they weren't returned to unit. You were only returned to unit if you did something drastically wrong, or you failed. But these didn't drop out. I was fit, because I had been a professional footballer [with Chesterfield F.C.] previous to joining.

We had two Shanghai policemen [Major William E. Fairbairn and Eric A. Sykes] come to teach unarmed combat.

Eric Anthony Sykes.

Major William Fairbairn.

Below right: Armed and ready for duty. Life in the Shanghai police was extremely tough and dangerous. Experience gained in Shanghai by Fairbairn and Sykes, proved invaluable in training the Commando in the art of unarmed combat.

Major Fairbairn demonstrating the use of his dagger.

COMMANDOS

We had a fighting knife. We were taught that when a man came for you, you knocked his arm across his body and then stepped forward so that he was behind you and then by using your thigh you threw him over your shoulder. He taught us that with a fighting knife you don't stab downwards you go in straight or upwards. But we never used those knives. It wasn't a knife that was used in my opinion. We just carried them; if we went on parade we had to have them.

IWM Sound Archive 22671 (2002)
Commandos practise one of the many martial arts moves shown to them by Fairbairn and Sykes.

Apart from showing aggression to the enemy, raising public morale at home and developing the necessary amphibious techniques for future, the Commando units were useful for specific tasks, operations where the dagger was more useful than the bludgeon. The airborne Bruneval raid, for example, when a Company of the 2nd Parachute Battalion dropped onto the French coast to grab an item of German radar equipment, was an operation that could not have been carried out in any other way. RAF bombers could have destroyed the radar site but the need was not to destroy the enemy equipment but bring it back to Britain and find out how it worked.

Circled: the German radar at Bruneval which was to be stolen in a raid conducted by a Company of the 2nd Parachute Battalion.

Operation Frankton, the Royal Marine canoe raid against German shipping in Bordeaux, satisfied a similar need. Again, RAF bombers could probably have sunk these ships but only at the cost of destroying a large part of the city and many French lives. As it was, five enemy ships were sunk for the loss of ten men, a viable cost in the circumstances.

During 1941, after quelling considerable opposition to the very idea of raiding operations in the War Office, some major raids were mounted, to the Lofoten Islands and the Norwegian port of Vaagso on December 27th. The Vaagso operation was a full-scale raid, with RAF bomber, a Royal Navy cruiser and four destroyers in close support, and demonstrated what a Commando force could do – not least in forcing the German to divert divisions from the Russian Front to protect the enemy held coast against more raids. The port installations were destroyed and a number of Germans were killed – but no Norwegians.

Commandos raiding the south-western coast of Norway at South Vaagso during 1941. Operations such as these were good morale boosters for the British Forces.

Commando raiders look on as valuable German oil supplies burn.

Frightened German captives are forced to pose for the camera whilst being prompted by their unwelcome guests.

Commandos celebrate another successful raid. Photographs like these showed the Germans that the British were able to fight back.

The same need, to destroy an enemy installation without causing loss of life among the civilian population was one of the motivations for the St. Nazaire raid. However this operation, like many others, had a strategic element that has often been forgotten – the need to limit the operational range of the German battleship *Tirpitz*, a warship that was tying up a large number of capital ships from the British Home Fleet, ships that the Royal Navy was anxious to employ on more useful duties.

Sister ship of the mighty *Bismarck*, sunk in 1940, the *Tirpitz* was a 'fleet in being', the most powerful battleship afloat; with her heavy guns and speed of 30 knots, and a range of 7,000 miles without refuelling, *Tirpitz* was a constant nightmare to the Allies. Those Allied warships she could not outfight she could outrun and if she broke out into the North Atlantic from her base in the Norwegian fjords, the damage she could do was thought to be incalculable.

To prevent such an occurrence, the Home Fleet kept a squadron ready at Scapa Flow and in the course of the war mounted several attacks, by the Fleet Air Arm, by Chariot human torpedoes and by midget submarines, all in an attempt to sink the *Tirpitz*. Some of these succeeded in damaging *Tirpitz* but she was not finally destroyed until December 1944, when Lancasters of No. 617 Squadron, RAF Bomber Command, ended her career.

The German battleship *Tirpitz* **undergoing camouflaging deep inside a Norwegian fjord.**

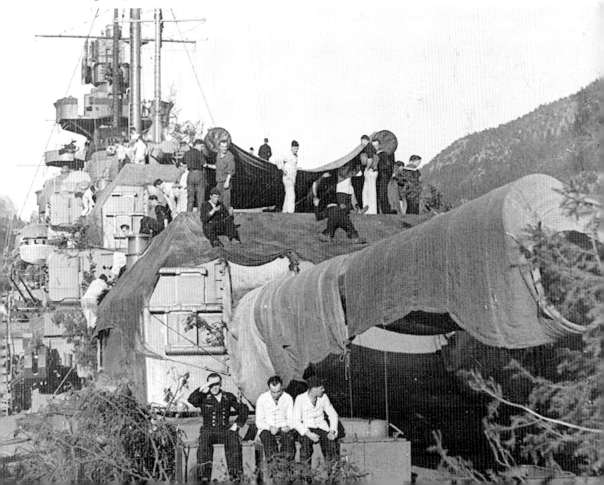

Above: the mighty Bismarck, *the scourge of the Royal Navy, and left: a photograph showing her immense size and weaponry she had at her disposal.*

These operations, however, lay in the future but in 1942 there was another fear. During her foray in 1940 *Bismarck* had been damaged by Fleet Air Arm torpedo aircraft and was heading for the French Breton coast when she was overtaken and sunk. Her destination was the port of St. Nazaire, in the estuary of the river Loire, because St. Nazaire contained a vast dry dock – the Forme Ecluse – the only dry dock on the Atlantic coast capable of receiving and repairing a ship the size of the *Bismarck* or the *Tirpitz*.

Here then was the rationale for the St. Nazaire raid; if the Forme Ecluse could be destroyed it would cause grave problems for the German Navy. If *Tirpitz* sailed and was damaged – and the Royal Navy would see to it that she was damaged – she could limp back to her Norwegian base where there were no repair facilities, attempt the run to the Baltic, or bolt for St. Nazaire and the Forme Ecluse.

Destroying the Forme Ecluse would be a major step in discouraging the Germans from deploying *Tirpitz* against the Atlantic or Russian convoys but how to achieve it? The Forme Ecluse was vast and in 1942 RAF bombing was inaccurate; at best the bombers might knock a few chips off the dockyard wall – and kill hundreds of French civilians in the process. Eventually, when all other possibilities had been examined and rejected, COHQ were asked to examine another possibility – a raid straight into the mouth of the Loire.

Could a Commando force - largely composed of sappers drawn from the Assault Engineer platoons of all the Commandos but protected by men of No. 2 Commando - sail up the Loire estuary in motor boats and on a converted destroyer stuffed with explosives, ram the dock gates, destroy the dock installations and render the Forme

Ecluse useless? The task was indeed formidable but it was accepted and planning began, though the hazards and dangers were fully recognized. *'There is certainly a VC in this'*, said one senior officer at COHQ In the end there were five – the hard-earned rewards of the 'Greatest Raid of All'.

'IT WASN'T REALLY SERIOUS SOLDIERING' - MEMORIES OF THE FIRST RAID – OPERATION COLLAR

By Sir Ronald Swayne MC Ex - Lieutenant, Herefordshire Regiment, 9 and 11 Independent Companies and finally 1 Commando

The origin of the Commandos was cooked up by Churchill… The idea was to send independent companies - they were to be called - to Norway to expand into guerrilla forces. And these were selected from various divisions, a brigade sending a platoon making three platoons from the division and a section from each battalion in the brigade with some Royal Engineers and RAMC.and signals, clerks and so on.

I was in the 38th Division, which was a Territorial Welsh border division. I was selected from my regiment, the Herefordshire Regiment, to take a section of Herefordshire boys, which I did, selecting lads who came from around my home really. And we went off and were formed into an Independent Company which was intended to get to Norway. But, by the time we were formed, the war was going very badly and although we got into a little passenger ship to go to Norway, we disembarked again and never went.

At the time of the retreat from Dunkirk… we suddenly got an instruction that some officers who could select their men were to report to …Southampton… and they were to take the most extraordinary combination of equipment including a sniper's rifle and this we did. And I suppose that was the real beginning of the Commandos.

The commanding officer was Colonel Ronnie Tod of the Argylls We had sixteen troops of eight men. It was a very strange formation and it was intended to make inroads immediately on the French coast… We trained very hard when we were there and eventually …we were told to go to a hotel in Whitehaven… We were there briefed by Jumbo Lester (sic) who was then a colonel, I think, a marine with a huge moustache. And Jumbo briefed us to go over in…a crash boat across the Channel. A crash boat's a small motor boat…built to pick up pilots when they ditched in the drink. It only did about eight knots and it didn't have room for more then about…twelve of us. I had three or four men who, armed to the teeth, were going to throw hand grenades and generally beat up a hotel in Merlimont Plage near Le Touquet…

We turned up rather late; it was almost beginning to get light. We went ashore and I went off to my objective with my men and we found it all boarded up... We wandered around a bit looking for Germans and then gave it up because time was running g out and went back and found there was no boat. The boat was hanging around off shore...And some Germans turned up whom we killed and that created a bit of noise. I'm afraid we bayoneted them. I hit one on the head with the butt of my revolver – wasn't very nice, it wasn't really serious soldiering. And of course because we were... rushed – it was unpardonable really - we never got their identity papers, which was very inefficient and we lost a lot of our weapons. I was armed with a .38 revolver. I'm sorry to say that I forgot to load it on this occasion. It was why I had to use the butt... but my batman bayoneted one and I grappled with the other and we killed them...We were under quite heavy fire when we withdrew and there was a lot of stuff flying around but they didn't hit anybody...We all got away safely.

Sir Ronald Swayne M.C., *The Commandos* IWM Sound Archive 10231/3 (1988)

ST NAZAIRE
OPERATION CHARIOT

A PLAN OF ELEGANT SIMPLICITY

By G. James Dorrian

James Dorrian is an acknowledged expert on the St. Nazaire raid. The results of his exhaustive research and interviews with veterans who provided first hand accounts of the raid were published in his book *Storming St. Nazaire* (Leo Cooper 1998).

When the *Tirpitz* moved into Norwegian waters in mid-January 1942, she prompted an immediate response in London, where all possible means were sought to close such doors as the British believed open to her. Aerial reconnaissance and signals intelligence continued to monitor her movements; the North Sea exits were patrolled; and a powerful battle-fleet based at Scapa Flow stood ready to intercept her should she attempt to undertake an anti-shipping sortie.

Reactive measures such as these could not, however, guarantee to prevent this great ship from posing an immediate threat to the vital Atlantic convoys - especially bearing in mind how vulnerable were operations in the North Sea to adverse weather conditions. All of which meant that, since Bomber

The mighty German Battleship, Tirpitz is towed into a fjord off Norway.

GREAT BRITAIN

Plymouth

Falmouth

*ENGLISH
CHANNEL*

Channel
Islands

Brest

Lorient

St Nazaire

F R A N C E

*ATLANTIC
OCEAN*

The Tirpitz in dry dock being fitted out during February 1940. This picture reveals the immense size of the ship's hull and emphasises the need for a vast dock required for refits.

Command seemed disinclined to mount an offensive against her defended anchorage, every effort had to be made to persuade her masters that the risks inherent in such an expedition were so extreme as to be insupportable.

Ironically the key to such a policy lay in the operational restrictions imposed by the sheer size of this class of warship: for only the giant Forme–Ecluse Louis-Joubert otherwise known as the *Normandie* dry dock in the French Atlantic port of St. Nazaire - the dock for whose shelter her sister-ship *Bismarck* had been steaming when caught and sunk - was capable of providing her with easily accessed repair facilities should she ever be damaged in battle. More than three football pitches long by fifty metres wide and sixteen metres deep, the dock had been specially built to hold the 80,000-ton *Normandie*, built in 1932. Destroy this one massive dock and *Tirpitz* would be left with no alternative but to attempt a hazardous return to Germany through a North Sea heavily patrolled by vigilant British air and naval assets.

Fortunately for the British, the port of St. Nazaire was anything but an unknown quantity, having been used as an entry point for expeditionary forces in both World Wars. As a consequence of this familiarity, the various services had amassed and shared a considerable body of intelligence relating to its dockyards, its repair facilities and its growing importance as a primary U-boat base. Following regular aerial surveys the RAF had constructed a detailed model to assist in targetting.

The vast Normandie dry dock, purposely built in 1932 to house the French 80,000 ton Normandie cruise liner. It was more than three football pitches long, fifty metres wide and sixteen metres deep.

St. Nazaire in peaceful times. Pictured here is the north end of Place du Bassin which was later to be the Commandos Group One Target.

Additional information about its defences and the structure of the U-boat pens had come from French sources. Perhaps most surprisingly of all, two sapper officers, Captains Bill Pritchard and Bob Montgomery, were found to have already developed a demolition plan for the harbour facilities as part of an unrelated engineering exercise aimed at demonstrating the vulnerability of docks in general to skilfully placed explosives.

With so much information to hand various planners had, since the fall of France, sought to capitalize on St. Nazaire's obvious potential as a raiding target. However,

German U-Boats and crews in St. Nazaire docks. From here U-Boat Flotillas were able patrol the Atlantic, harrassing the British Merchant fleet.

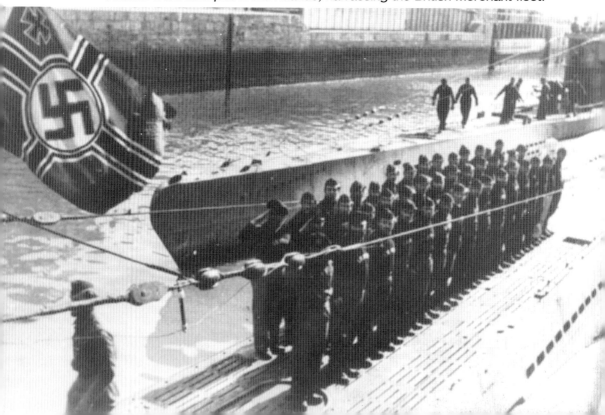

by the early months of 1942 none had yet come up with a solution to the particular natural defences which, on the face of it, seemed to render the port immune from seaward attack: for St. Nazaire was situated six miles inside the estuary of the River Loire, and its approaches were protected by shoals and mud-flats so extensive as to restrict any warship to the narrow, deep-water channel which ran right beneath the gun batteries ranged along the estuary's northern shore.

Well concealed U-Boats in their pens in St. Nazaire. The RAF had tried and failed many times to destroy these facilities from the air.

With all previous attempts having failed, the task of producing a workable plan of attack might have been thought something of a poisoned chalice when, on 27th January, following a meeting between Churchill and Admiral of the Fleet Sir Dudley Pound, it was passed on to Commodore the Lord

Above & below: the Combined Operations Badge and Lord Louis Mountbatten, recent apointee to the post of Adviser on Combined Operations.

Louis Mountbatten and his Combined Operations HQ. A relatively recent appointee to the post of Adviser on Combined Operations, the charismatic Mountbatten had been charged with creating the organisation that would eventually pave the way for a victorious return to mainland Europe. It is important to note, however, that in January 1942 the concept of the primary services 'combining' for the common good was still considerably more aspirational than reflective of the fact that they were about to forego their traditional, and much cherished, independence.

Headquartered at Richmond Terrace in London, COHQ had at its disposal the Commandos of Brigadier Joseph Haydon's Special Service Brigade but, with the exception of these elite troops it commanded no forces of its own and therefore relied for its effectiveness on the co-operation and goodwill of Navy, Army and Air Force. Short of both men and material, the organisation was nevertheless blessed by the inventiveness of its planning staff who, by the time the problem had been passed to Mountbatten, had on their own account already spotted a potential chink in their target's armour. It was all to do with an approaching alignment of sun, moon and earth,

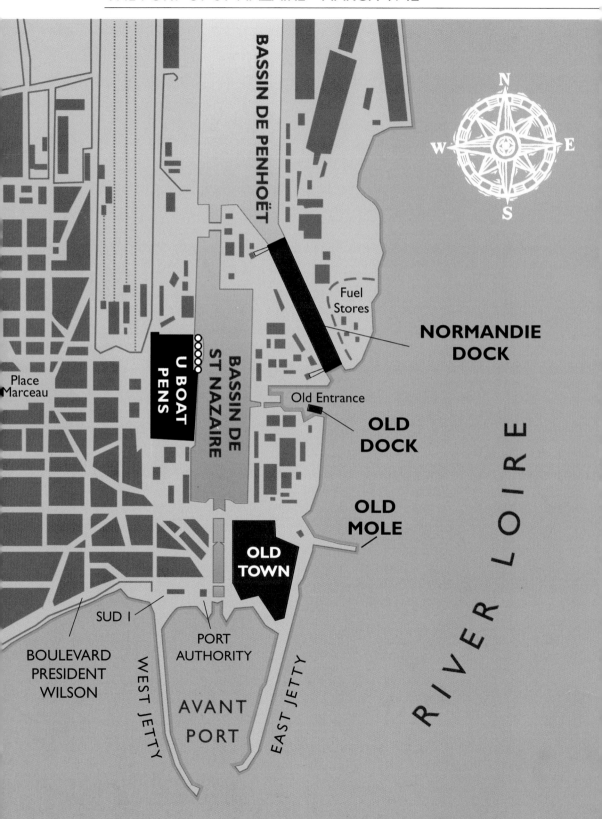

BASSIN DE PENHOËT

Fuel Stores

NORMANDIE DOCK

U BOAT PENS

BASSIN DE ST NAZAIRE

Place Marceau

Old Entrance

OLD DOCK

OLD MOLE

OLD TOWN

SUD I

PORT AUTHORITY

BOULEVARD PRESIDENT WILSON

WEST JETTY

AVANT PORT

EAST JETTY

RIVER LOIRE

One of the huge Normandie *dock caissons - a nine metre wide hollow gate. These were to be the Combined Operations main target, a task that was to test the skills of Captain John Hughes-Hallett.*

which, during the last days of March would cause exceptionally high tides to flood the estuary of the Loire. Were a suitable force to be ready in time, then vessels of lighter draught would be able to avoid the deep-water channel and attack instead across the very shallows upon which the enemy relied for protection. Such an approach would, of necessity, be particularly time sensitive and, having got an attacking force in on the flood tide, there would be the thorny problem of getting them out again as it ebbed.

Instructed by Mountbatten to formulate proposals for submission to higher authority, it took little more than a week for a team lead by his Naval Adviser, Captain John Hughes-Hallett, to produce a plan of elegant simplicity. Two specially lightened destroyers, carrying between them a strong Commando force, would approach the port across the shallows. One of the ships, fitted with a large explosive charge, would ram the outer caisson – a nine metre wide, hollow gate that could be wound into the dock's west wall - of the *Normandie* dock and disgorge her troops onto the dockside before blowing up after a short delay. In conjunction with troops landed elsewhere by the second destroyer, these would complete a number of important demolition tasks on shore before survivors, along with the crew of the ramming ship, re-embarked for the long voyage home. Having destroyed the outer caisson, a specially modified Motor Torpedo Boat (MTB) would enter the dry dock and torpedo the inner gate. Of crucial importance was the projected contribution of Bomber Command, whose aircraft would divert the attention of German gunners by attacking adjacent areas. Put up to the Admiralty, on 7th February as the most effective way of achieving the result they themselves desired, the proposal was met by an absolute refusal to commit any British destroyers to such an enterprise.

Between 7th February and the end of the month, various attempts were made to

MTB 74, a modified motor boat used for attacking battle cruisers. One of these was to enter the dry dock and torpedo the inner caisson.

The USS Buchanan *later to become HMS* Campbeltown.

overcome this potentially crippling decision. The possible use of a French destroyer was soon abandoned when it became clear that, for security reasons, the French were not to be told of the raid. The employment of a submarine as ramming ship did not survive the realisation that it would be too small and light to have any effect on the massive caisson. And fortunately for all concerned, the rather desperate alternative of mounting an attack with sixty-five ton, wooden-hulled Fairmile 'B' Motor Launches (MLs), unsupported by any heavy ship, also failed to overcome serious scrutiny.

In the event it was Mountbatten himself who solved the problem by threatening outright cancellation if no suitable vessel could be made available by 3rd March and faced with such an ultimatum, the Admiralty finally conceded defeat and earmarked an elderly WW1 American destroyer now sailing under British colours as HMS *Campbeltown* as lead ship for the raid. But this was as far as they were prepared to go. There would be no second heavy ship. Instead, *Campbeltown* would sail to meet the enemy supported only by a dozen of the Fairmiles - flimsy vessels drawn from Coastal Forces, which in action would prove entirely unsuited to the role of assault ships.

The flimsy wooden hulled Fairmile 'B' Motor Launch. These were assigned to support the Campbeltown *during the assault.*

**Lieutenant Colonel A.C. Newman,
2 Commando.**

Commander Robert Ryder.

For some time, therefore, the fate of the raid had hung in the balance. Yet in spite of this the COHQ planners had forged ahead with the assembly of resources, the training of personnel and the appointment of the two officers who, as Military and Naval Force Commanders respectively, would share overall control of the operation. In filling the first post the providential choice was Lieutenant Colonel Charles Newman, CO of No. 2 Commando. He would construct his plan of attack in close collaboration with Commander Robert Ryder, RN, who was detailed to act as his naval opposite number.

A territorial officer of thirty-seven, Newman was faced with the daunting task of engineering an opposed landing and executing a comprehensive catalogue of demolition tasks on shore - all within a time-scale dictated by the fact that his men would have no support beyond the weapons, explosives and ammunition they could carry with them. Bearing in mind that there would quickly come a point beyond which his men would not be able to resist a strengthening enemy, Newman therefore required that all demolition tasks be completed within thirty minutes of landing and that all parties be on board the boats and on their way home again only ninety minutes after that.

To make all this possible, activities on shore would have to be carefully choreographed. Landing in three groups, from Fairmiles at the Old Mole and Old Entrance, and from *Campbeltown* directly onto the caisson, the attacking force would be broken down into parties with very specific functions. 'Assault' troops would storm ashore first to overwhelm local defences and establish a secure perimeter. Landing behind these would be teams of 'Demolition' specialists, each of whose activities would be covered by heavily armed 'Protection' squads.

Group 1 objective, The Old Mole. This lighthouse was to be the primary re-embarkation point.

GROUP ONE TARGETS

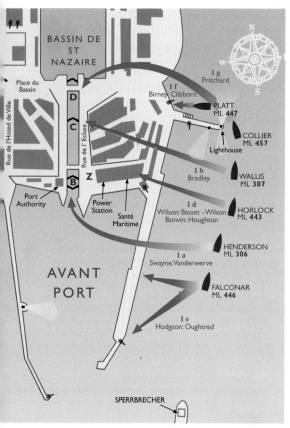

GROUP 1,

Commanded by Captain Bertie Hodgson, the parties in this group were to secure the heavily defended Old Mole and hold it as a primary re-embarkation point clear the area of the Old Town, destroy the power station complex and demolish the gates and bridges spanning the New Entrance lock.

GROUP 2

Further to the north the parties under Captain Micky Burn's command were to land in the Old Entrance, clear the warehouse area between there and the Mole and clear and hold the all-important block of land between the Normandie dock and the Submarine Basin. In order to isolate this area from the main town, the Pont de la Douane was to be blown early on, followed by the Old Entrance crossings once all northern parties had withdrawn toward the re-embarkation point.

GROUP 3

Storming ashore from *Campbeltown* herself, Major Bill Copland's parties were to complete the neutralization of the great dock by destroying the north caisson, both winding houses and the pumping station. Should it prove possible, the underground fuel stores east of the dock were to be fired by the 'Assault' party disembarking to starboard.

With *Campbeltown* securely wedged in the caisson and her scuttling charges activated, her crew were to board two of the MLs for the journey home. Having landed all their troops as planned the remaining Fairmiles were to stand off the Old Mole to be loaded with retiring Commandos as instructed by the Naval Piermaster Lieutenant Verity, RNVR.

Reflecting the difference in skills that would be required on the night, the training of the demolition specialists was taking place independently of the fighting troops who would make up the 'Assault' and 'Protection'

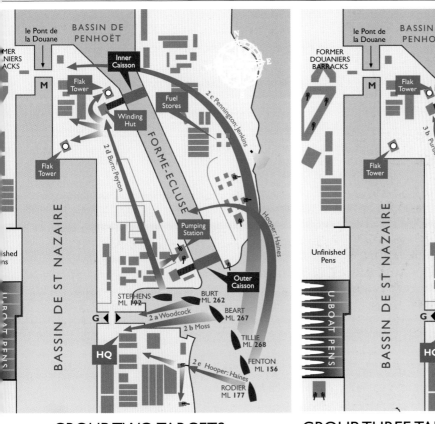

GROUP TWO TARGETS

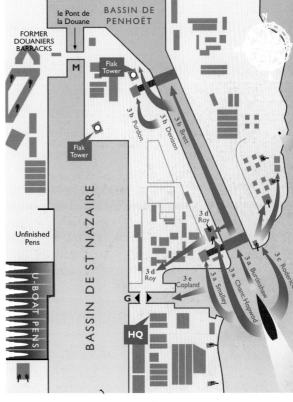

GROUP THREE TARGETS

Major Bill Copland, DSO, 2 Commando.

parties. Drawn from Nos. 1,2,3,4,5,6,9 and 12 Commandos, these had come together during the latter part of February in the Scottish port of Burntisland, there to be instructed in the art of dockyard demolition by Captains Pritchard and Montgomery. At the end of the month the parties would move on to complete their training at Barry Docks in Cardiff and in Southampton, whose King George V dock so closely mirrored the structure of their target in St. Nazaire.

As for the fighting troops, these represented the very best of Newman's own No. 2 Commando, a unit which had only just returned to its base in Ayr from landing exercises in the Outer Hebrides when he was summoned to take up his new post in London. With Newman absent, the actual selection of men was delegated to his second-in-command, Major Bill Copland, a veteran of the 1917 Battle of Passchendaele who, during much of the planning phase, would continue to drill them thoroughly in the black art of street fighting by night.

35

*Torpedo specialist
Lieutenant Nigel
Tibbits.*

In contrast to the resources available to Copland and Newman, Commander Ryder found himself in the position of having to organize a major assault on an enemy port with no staff, no administrative structure and, until such time as *Campbeltown* belatedly arrived on the scene, no ramming ship. A career naval officer of thirty-four, he had been serving as Naval Liaison to the Headquarters of the Army's Southern Command, when summoned on 25th February to take part in 'Chariot', just three days after Newman. Indeed, having arrived late at the planning meeting of the 26th, where the details of the various appointments were to be made known, he had accepted his new role without actually knowing who, or what force, he was to command. With only one month to go before the tidal surge that would make the operation possible, he was therefore having to start from scratch, his already daunting task exacerbated by the antagonism which at that time characterized relations between COHQ and the Admiralty.

Having discussed, in concert with Newman, the various unsatisfactory alternatives to the use of a destroyer, the last minute provision of *Campbeltown* came as a huge relief to Ryder. In fact she arrived on the scene just in time to become the centrepiece of a planning meeting held on 3rd March, at which clearance was given for both Force Commanders to draw up their orders in detail. Amongst other issues resolved at this time were the provision of a submarine to stand off the estuary mouth and act as a final navigational beacon, and confirmation that the Cornish port of Falmouth would be the venue for the assembly and training of the naval force, with a view to departure for St. Nazaire on the 27th. The torpedo specialist, Lieutenant Nigel Tibbits, RN, was tasked with transforming *Campbeltown* into a floating bomb, for which purpose she was to be sailed without delay to Devonport dockyard. Before joining the other ships she would be rearmed with Oerlikon 20 mm cannon, fitted with armour protection and structurally modified to resemble a German ship of the *Möwe* class. While in Devonport every effort would be made to reduce her draught, but absolutely no guarantee could be given of a safe passage across the estuary shoals.

Weighing against the generally positive tone of the meeting was the RAF's refusal to accede to Newman's request for close air support with a view to the direct suppression of enemy fire. Bearing in mind that the success of the raid had been largely predicated on the ability of Bomber Command to divert the enemy's attention away from the seaward approaches to St. Nazaire, their perceived vacillation at so late a stage was a perplexing and worrying development.

On Friday 6th March, Ryder reported to the C-in-C Plymouth, Admiral of the Fleet Sir Charles Forbes. As commander of the coastal sector from which the force would depart, Forbes was to be 'Patron' of the operation and as such his attitude toward it was likely to be of particular significance. Having earlier failed, on his own account, to come up with a solution to the many problems posed by targeting St. Nazaire, Forbes had been quick to caution Mountbatten that in pushing ahead he risked losing all, or most, of his men and ships. Yet in spite of his deep personal

Lieutenant Commander Sam Beattie, he was to be appointed Captain of the *Campbeltown*.

Lieutenant Dunstan Curtis, Commander of Motor Gun Boat 314 which was to be assigned as the fleet headquarters ship.

misgivings Ryder was to find in him a level of support and co-operation not always evident in his dealings with the authorities in London.

Four days later Ryder was joined by Newman and his adjutant, Captain Stanley Day, for a conference hosted by Forbes which brought together most of the key naval personnel. Learning of the raid for the first time was Lieutenant Commander Sam Beattie, the newly appointed captain of *Campbeltown*. Added to the team by virtue of their specialist skills, were Lieutenant Bill Green, as Force Navigator, and Sub Lieutenant O'Rourke, as Signals Officer. Pritchard and Tibbits were there to outline their demolition plans for the dockyard and *Campbeltown* respectively. Also attending were Lieutenant Commander Billie Stephens, CO.of the 20th M.L. Flotilla, who would act as Senior Officer ML's; Lieutenant Commander Wood, CO of the 28th ML Flotilla; Lieutenant Dunstan Curtis, CO of Motor Gun Boat (MGB) 314, the gunboat which had been added to the fleet to act as headquarters ship; and Sub Lieutenant Micky Wynn, CO of MTB 74, the boat whose specially modified torpedoes were to supplement *Campbeltown*'s charge, or indeed replace it should the destroyer for any reason fail to ram.

A primary consideration of the conference was to establish a course to St. Nazaire that would avoid enemy air patrols. This was determined largely on the basis of material provided by the Admiralty's own Operational Intelligence Centre, in conjunction with information supplied by Air Intelligence. In its final form the chosen route would take the force on a voyage of some 450 miles, travelling deep into the Bay of Biscay before turning sharply north of east for the final run to the estuary mouth. Also resolved were issues relating to security, and the date and form of a mock attack on Devonport whose purpose would be to gauge the force's true state of readiness.

At the conclusion of the various discussions Newman returned briefly to London, while Ryder established himself in Falmouth prior to the arrival of the first MLs. To conceal their true purpose and provide legitimate cover for the training activities that would characterize the final weeks, he set up a wholly fictitious body known as the 'Tenth Anti-Submarine Striking Force', with himself as Senior Officer. The concept of sweeps deep into enemy waters was considered sufficient justification for modifications made to the MLs, each of which was to be fitted with long-range deck tanks, and two single Oerlikon mountings to replace their standard fit of an elderly 3-pounder forward.

On 12th March the operation at last began to assume a physical form with the arrival of the MLs Four of these – MLs 192, 262, 267, and 268, were from Stephens' 20th Flotilla, the remaining eight – MLs 298, 306, 307, 341, 443, 446, 447, and 457 - representing the full complement of Wood's 28th Flotilla. An important day in the chronology of the raid, the 12th also saw the fighting troops of 2 Commando prepare to sail from Ayr to Falmouth on board the commando ship *Princess Josephine Charlotte*. (*PJC*) Arriving in port on the 13th, these would be joined by the demolition teams who, having also completed their training, had travelled overnight from Cardiff by train.

At last it was Newman's turn to quit the capital and join his men. As he exited COHQ for the last time, he received from Mountbatten the chastening advice that, while the operation upon which he was about to embark was of great strategic importance, it might well exact a bitter toll in terms of casualties; and this being the case, Newman should feel free to offer those with family ties or serious misgivings, the opportunity of opting out without being thought any the worse for doing so. Having stayed overnight in Tavistock, he arrived on board the *PJC* on the 14th, carrying with him a treasure-trove of material. Included in this was the RAF's scale model of the port, the latest aerial photos of the target, four of the newest type of wireless set and a draft of his orders in detail.

Also arriving on the 14th was MTB 74. This sleek vessel had originally been earmarked for a daring attack on the battlecruisers *Scharnhorst* and *Gneisenau* in Brest harbour, the idea being that she should fire motorless explosive-packed torpedoes over the nets protecting the ships, from tubes mounted high on her foredeck. Robbed of her purpose by the battlecruisers' successful dash through the

FAIRMILE TYPE B MOTOR LAUNCH (ML) - PRIOR TO CONVERSION

Camouflaged in Mountbatten (Plymouth) Pink

Dimensions: 112 x 18¼ x 4¼ ft • **Displacement:** 73 tons
Engines: 2 shaft 600hp each Hall-Scott petrol motors
Speed: 20 knots at 2,200 rpm - 16.7 knots at 1,800 rpm
Fuel: 2,305 gallons • **Range:** 1,500 miles at 12 knots
Guns: 3pdr - 20mm Oerlikon - 2 machine guns

Illustration by Jon Wilkinson.

VICKERS
2 POUNDER
POM POM

VICKERS
MACHINE
GUNS

ROLLS ROYCE
2 POUNDER

Illustration by Jon Wilkinson.

Channel in February, her special weapons were now to be employed in support of *Campbeltown*.

On the 16th, commando fortitude was put to the test when the troops boarded the MLs for a shakedown cruise out into the Atlantic. Initially scheduled to last for thirty-six hours, it was curtailed by severe gales which forced the fleet to shelter overnight in the Scilly Isles. Most of the men were violently seasick and the lesson was quickly learned that an attack in other than calm conditions would be out of the question.

Almost inevitably the final weeks saw a steady accretion of men and ships as particular needs were identified and catered for. The total of personnel to be carried would eventually grow to include journalists, native French and German speakers, Intelligence representatives, Flotilla base engineers, additional medical orderlies - even staff from Newman's own HQ. In respect of the fleet itself the priority was to supplement the fire of the lightly-armed MLs by adding a strike-force capable of engaging enemy ships in, or close to, the estuary. Two destroyers had already been added as passage escorts but, as these were to remain on patrol well off the enemy shore, the actual raiding force was strengthened by the addition of four torpedo MLs from the 7th Flotilla at Dartmouth.

With Commando shore leave cancelled, and all troops safely back on board the *PJC*, Newman began his briefings informing the officers on the 18th and the remainder of the men on the 19th, of specific details which, at this point, excluded a precise identification of their target. The high morale of all concerned was reflected in the fact that no one chose to accept his offer of exclusion without prejudice to character. Ryder would not commence his briefing of naval COs and First Lieutenants until the 23rd. In contrast to the military personnel the remaining naval officers and ratings would remain ignorant of the task awaiting them until after the force had sailed.

The 18th saw the arrival of the gunboat which would carry Newman and Ryder into the estuary, along with the Dartmouth boats – MLs 156, 160, 177, and 270. Having been added to the force at such a late stage, there would not be time to fit them with Oerlikons, which meant they must rely instead on the fire of their obsolete 3-pounders.

With the full force of sixteen MLs now assembled, it was time to execute 'Vivid', the rehearsal attack on Devonport. Conducted under the pretext of an exercise to test the defences of Plymouth and Devonport, this took place over the night of the 21st-22nd and transpired to be something of a fiasco. Almost everything went wrong. The radios refused to work and men were either landed in the wrong place or not at all. Ryder saw the sorry affair as a useful learning experience, but Forbes, watching from the shore, must have seen in it the potential fruition of all his worst fears.

Adding to the two Commanders' share of worries was the clear indication that, with only days to go, their vital air plan seemed close to the point of collapse. Originally seen as a substantial umbrella under the shelter of which the fleet might slip unnoticed

The Oerlikon 20mm Anti Aircraft gun. These were a Swiss design and proved to be hard hitting long range weapons. Illustrated by Jon Wilkinson.

into the estuary, the number of bombers to be employed had fallen from a desired 350 or so, to a mere 62. To make matters still worse, the stipulation that much of the bombing be directed at parts of the town immediately adjacent to the dockyard had fallen foul of a political decision aimed at minimizing French civilian casualties. Such aircraft as Bomber Command now felt able to commit would therefore be obliged to direct their efforts at areas too far from the landing places to do more than ensure that German gun-crews would be on high alert when the British ships arrived in port.

HMS *Tynedale* and HMS *Atherstone*, the Hunt-class destroyers detailed as passage escorts arrived in Falmouth on the 23rd. Presented at last with an opportunity to transfer his headquarters away from the seafront hotel which had

HMS Atherstone a Hunt-Class destroyer chosen to escort the fleet to the Loire estuary.

HMS Tynedale.

served since his arrival, Ryder lost no time in moving himself and his staff to the latter ship.

HMS *Campbeltown*, her modifications now completed, sailed in on the 25th. So as to resemble a German boat and, in conjunction with spurious signals, assist in concealing the forces' true identity from the port's defenders, two of her four funnels had been removed, and the remaining two cut back at an angle. Gone was her usual armament of 4-inch guns, to be replaced by Oerlikon cannon ranged along each flank, and a solitary 12-pounder on her foredeck. Her bridge structure now had armour protection and low armoured screens had been attached to the deck amidships to protect the commando parties who would be lying in the open during her final approach. At her heart was the huge explosive charge designed by Tibbits in collaboration with Pritchard. Consisting of

The Campbeltown *at various stages of conversion, being fitted with armoured screens, sloping funnels, Oerlikon cannon along her flanks and a 12-pounder on the foredeck.*

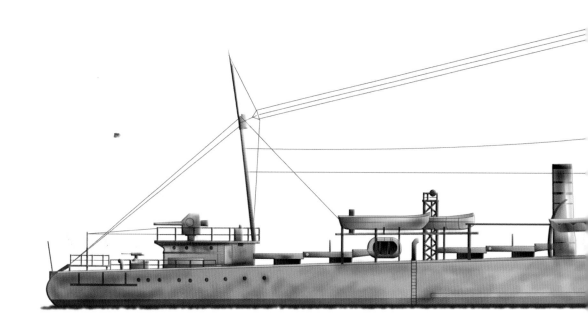

CAMPBELTOWN'S MODIFICATIONS

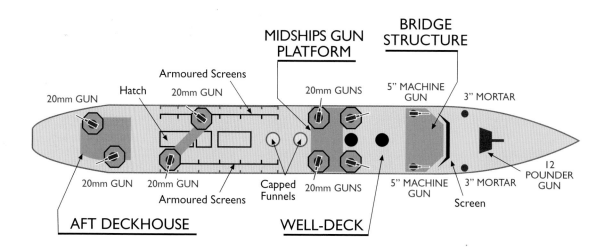

BRIDGE
STRUCTURE

MIDSHIPS GUN
PLATFORM

Armoured Screens

20mm GUN · Hatch · 20mm GUN · 20mm GUNS · 5" MACHINE
GUN · 3" MORTAR

AFT DECKHOUSE

20mm GUN · 20mm GUN · Capped Funnels · 20mm GUNS · 5" MACHINE
GUN · 3" MORTAR · Screen

Armoured Screens

12
POUNDER
GUN

WELL-DECK

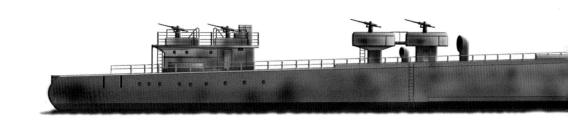

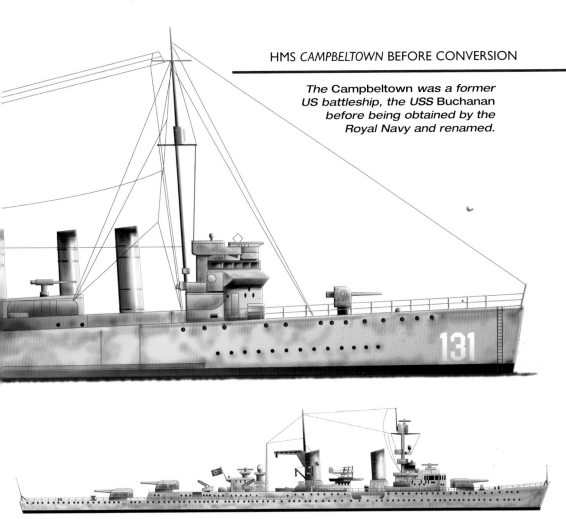

HMS *CAMPBELTOWN* BEFORE CONVERSION

The **Campbeltown** *was a former US battleship, the USS* Buchanan *before being obtained by the Royal Navy and renamed.*

131

A profile of a two funnelled German destroyer. The **Campbeltown** was refitted to imitate an enemy vessel in order to fool the Germans as she sailed up the Loire estuary.

HMS *CAMPBELTOWN* AFTER CONVERSION

Painted in Plymouth pink, minus two funnels and fitted with amoured screens to protect the Commando raiding parties. The refit took place at Devonport and was completed in 15 days.

Illustrations by Jon Wilkinson.

Captain Micky Burn, 6 Troop, 2 Commando.

twenty-four Mk VII depth charges, it was concealed in a special compartment built into the bow immediately abaft the forward gun support. Weighing four and a quarter tons, it was fitted with a variety of delayed-action fuses whose purpose was to ensure an explosion whatever the circumstances.

With all his ships now in port and so as to take advantage of favourable weather, Ryder obtained permission to sail on the 26th. To maintain the illusion of an anti-submarine force, the ships would assume a broad sweep formation while sailing during daylight hours. The MLs were now capable of making the return journey under their own steam, but the shorter range MGB and MTB would have to be towed behind *Atherstone* and *Campbeltown* respectively. Only when close to the enemy shore and after parting company with the Hunts would the force deploy into its attack formation of two parallel columns flanking *Campbeltown* on either side. To port of the destroyer would be six MLs of Wood's flotilla carrying Captain Hodgson's Group 1, and to starboard six MLs led by Stephens and carrying Captain Burn's Group 2. At the head of each column would be a torpedo-ML, ready to engage enemy ships. The gunboat, with Newman and Ryder on board would lead the whole formation, with two spare M.L.s and the skittish MTB bringing up the rear.

Almost at the very last moment aerial photos revealed the presence of five German torpedo boats - of a similar tonnage to the Hunts - in the Submarine Basin close to the building Newman had earmarked for his HQ. It had been known beforehand that these boats were active on the Biscay coast, and Forbes had arranged to keep Ryder apprised of their position. Their sudden appearance right in the heart of the landing area was a potentially deadly development, yet the decision to push ahead with the raid was amended only by an appeal to Forbes for whatever naval reinforcements could be made available at such short notice. Inevitably the result was a compromise in that two additional destroyers might be provided - but too late to sail with the main force. In this case the best that could be hoped for was a later rendezvous somewhere close to the target area.

On the morning of the 26th, a final flurry of activity saw the commandos and the last of their equipment loaded onto *Campbeltown* and the troop-carrying MLs. A total of 269 men, including odds and sods, were distributed between the ships with the MLs carrying some 15 troops apiece. At 12:30 hours the executive order 'Carry out CHARIOT' was received from Forbes' HQ and shortly thereafter the formation prepared to sail out of port - but without Lieutenant Commander Wood, who had been taken seriously ill just 15 minutes before the off. This was a serious blow to Ryder who, in the absence of a suitable replacement, would now have no alternative but to engineer a reassignment of command duties while his force was at sea.

'THE WHOLE THING WAS BEAUTIFULLY PLANNED'

By Sir Ronald Swayne MC Ex - Lieutenant, Herefordshire Regiment, 9 and 11 Independent Companies, No. 1 Special Service Battalion and finally No. 1 Commando

My Independent Company was put into 'A' Company, No. 1 Special Service battalion...About April 1941 we were moved up to Achnacarry...And we were pulling together and becoming much more professional and at that time we were turned into No. 1 Commando.

The Commandos tended to be clubs...each Commando had its own character. No. 3 Commando - which I think was one of the Commandos which was efficient very early on - was mostly regular officers and regular soldiers. I think my Commando was a good Commando so far as training was concerned. No. 2 Commando was London based Territorial, London and Essex. That was the Commando that formed the main force for St. Nazaire; very high rate of intelligence and quality, both officers and men. In fact, a lot of the men, if they hadn't been taken prisoner, would have become officers and some of those who got home became officers later. They were very good. In a Commando like No. 2 it was much more like a well-run public school. I mean they were put more on their honour, tough discipline wasn't necessary. In my Commando there was a lot of very tough discipline.

I first heard of [the raid] when I had just been married and my wife and I were with No. 1 Commando in Irving. I was selected to take a detachment of twelve from No. 1 Commando - all to be a demolition group to join No. 2 Commando under Colonel Newman - and various detachments who were trained in demolitions from other Commandos...training on blowing up docks. I went to Scotland to Burntisland. My sergeant, Tom Durrant who was killed and got the VC, was put in charge as temporary RSM for the party. I was only a subaltern. Bill Pritchard said I was to take charge of the administration. I made rather a mess of it because we lost a lot of blankets.

We practised blowing up pumping stations and locks in Leith and Rosyth and Edinburgh, based at Burntisland. Then I was sent down to Cardiff, to prepare for our reception by the Welch Regiment and we went into barracks. This wasn't the whole lot. There was another detachment doing the same thing in Southampton. The officers lived in the Angel Hotel or digs and the troops were in the Welch Regiment depot and we practised blowing up Pontypool, Newport and Cardiff. We learnt how to lower sacks of explosive against the lock gates at the point where it would do the most damage. And we learnt how to deal with these big, metal caissons - empty, narrow chambers which slot into the locks. And also pumping machinery: the impeller pumps and machinery

45

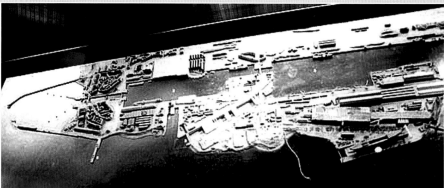

The model of St. Nazaire and the Normandie *dock used to brief the Commandos.*

required to empty a lock and to transfer water in a lock system. We did that for long enough to turn the groups of soldiers into really efficient teams, knowing exactly what each man had to do... then we went on down to Falmouth and joined the ship [Princess Josephine Charlotte]. We were shut up there; we weren't allowed to go ashore. Then we were assembled by Colonel Newman, who outlined the purpose and planning for the raid and gave us a rough idea of our tasks and about forty pages of orders. I went off to the lavatory, as the only really quiet place in the ship, to read my orders. I'm terribly forgetful - and there was furious knocking on the door after about ten minutes and I hurried up and left to find the colonel outside and went back to my cabin. To my horror I found that I'd left the orders in the lavatory. I got the biggest ticking off I'd ever had in my life!

It was very well planned. We had all the information we needed. We had a model of St. Nazaire which gave us an absolutely clear idea of what we had to do, where our targets were, how to get there, where the enemy might be, what support we were getting from our little support groups. I was to blow up the southern lock on the new entrance, that big, long...main entance to the port. I think there were two locks there we had to blow up and a swing bridge. I had eight men and a detachment under John Vanderwerve, officer in No. 2 Commando with four soldiers armed with Tommy guns to protect us while we did this...

We really knew exactly what to do by the time we left...the whole thing was beautifully planned. Equipment was good, we had exactly, very well thought out loads of explosive to carry and the arming was very good. We had Tommy guns and Remington Colts...Trouble is the Remington Colt's a wonderful weapon but you need to learn how to use it and my demolition soldiers were armed with this beautiful weapon but they really didn't know how to use it.

My Sergeant, Tom Durrant, was a very good shot. Actually, I'm boasting, but he and I were the best shots in the Commando, we could beat 'em all at rifle shooting. But he was a very good shot with a pistol too.

Sir Ronald Swayne M.C., *The Commandos* IWM Sound Archive 10231/3 (1988)

THE VOYAGE

Ryder's fleet of MLs left the safe haven of Falmouth at 2.00 p.m. on the 26th and sailed into the English Channel in two columns at 13 knots. *Campbeltown*, *Atherstone* and *Tynedale* followed on an hour later. Leading the convoy - arranged in a modified version of his Night Cruising Order - wide of the Lizard to avoid attracting the attention of curious eyes on the Cornish Coast, Ryder, aboard the *Atherstone*, with his co-commander Lieutenant Colonel Newman, adopted a south westerly heading and pushed on towards open water and point 'A' as per his route orders. Butting along in tow behind the *Atherstone* was MGB 314, the HQ boat, followed by *Tynedale* and then *Campbeltown* herself towing the MTB. The rest of the MLs formed two further columns on either side of the central column of destroyers. It was the first time all 21 vessels had sailed in formation as a single unit.

Under a comforting cover of haze induced by the warm spring sunshine the fleet then reduced its speed and shook out into 'Cruising Order No. 1', a broad arrowhead formation, with the MLs forming the arrowhead, to simulate an anti-submarine sweep. Ryder then juggled with the problem of command duties forced on him by Lieutenant Commander Wood's sudden and untimely illness. Ryder's 'spare' commanding officer, Lieutenant Horlock RNVR, took over command of ML 443 to replace Lieutenant Platt, who had assumed Wood's mantle in leading the port column aboard ML 447.

A little after 7.00p.m., with night approaching, the fleet reached point 'A' and Ryder ordered a course due south which would take them deep into the Bay of Biscay before the next stage of their approach to the mouth of the Loire. Increasing speed to 14 knots as the darkness enveloped it, the fleet adopted Night Cruising Order with parallel columns of MLs stationed either side of the three destroyers. It passed Point 'B' four hours later and changed course slightly to a heading which took it just east of south, aiming for Point 'C' at which they would begin their slow turn towards the hostile coast. To Ryder's dismay 27th March dawned in a blaze of brilliant light under a cloudless sky with visibility uninterrupted as far as the horizon. Nevertheless spirits were raised a little when the three destroyers hoisted the German ensign as part of their deception plan.

At around 7.00 a.m. the fleet reached point 'C' 160 miles west of St. Nazaire and resumed its simulation of an anti-submarine sweep. Once again the course was adjusted; now the heading was south east to begin the long run in towards its final destination.

Minutes later, a sharp-eyed gunner on the *Tynedale* noticed an object on the surface off to port some seven miles distant. Was it a German submarine? If so she might signal a sighting and elicit a response from the German Navy or worse, the *Luftwaffe* in which case the mission would be seriously compromised. Ryder's worst fears were realised with the confirmation of contact with a German U-Boat - later confirmed as U-593. This new but damaged vessel, ironically also headed for St. Nazaire for repairs, had been keeping a careful, yet uncertain eye on the Chariot force for some time. There was nothing for it but to sink her or at least force her into a dive before she could warn the German commanders ashore. *Tynedale* was ordered to engage, which she did at speed and with venom. Hoisting her White Ensign she fired the first of several salvoes at 7.45 a.m. driving the U-Boat beneath the surface in a crash dive, whilst Ryder himself set off in *Atherstone* to investigate two fishing boats in the vicinity. *Tynedale* steamed towards the point of the last sighting. The submarine, hoping to mount an attack of its own, broke the surface again but failed

Crewmen manning the Director Tower of HMS Tyndale *on the afternoon of 27th March 1943.*

A fearsome sight for British sailors. The sillhouette of the German U-593, which spotted the Chariot attack force.

to launch a stern torpedo. Frantically her captain dived once more to escape. Too close to the submarine to seed a full pattern of depth charges, *Tynedale* sped away to give herself room for manoeuvre but U-593 slipped away. She was not seen again.

At 9.30 a.m. the search was broken off. Unaware that the U-Boat had eluded him, several questions crowded in on Ryder's mind. Had she spotted his force? Had she been destroyed? He could not be sure. If the submarine had noted the presence and course of the MLs as well as the destroyers and had managed to get a signal off to the German Naval Commander in Chief in the West then the Chariot force was in jeopardy. Ryder's response to this possibility was as wise as it was decisive. *Tynedale* and *Atherstone* were ordered to change course and steam away to the southwest, to shake the submarine off the scent just in case U-593's periscope was still busily scanning the surface. After the war it transpired that the submarine had in fact noted MLs in Ryder's fleet and had relayed the same in a message to base, albeit some five hours after the initial contact. Although the U-Boat had not

German crewmen observe the sea from the flak tower of U-593 whilst on a patrol .

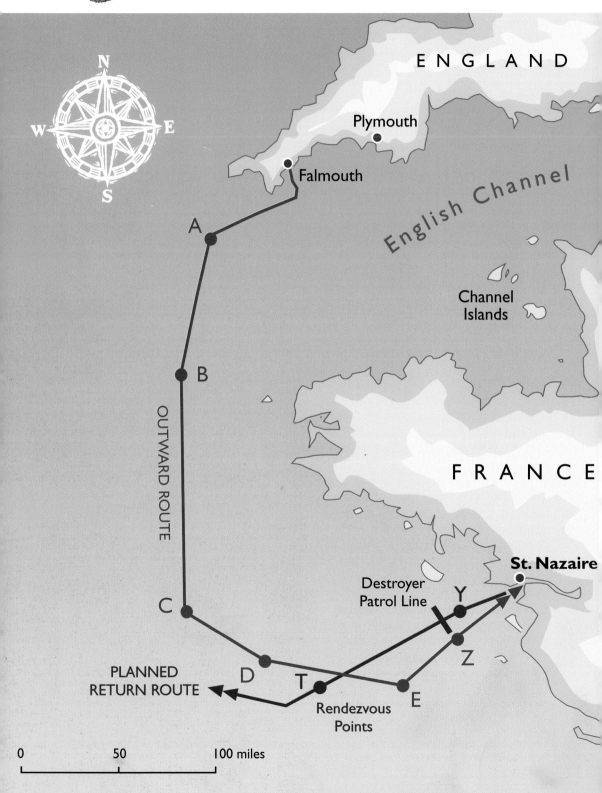

ENGLAND

Plymouth

Falmouth

English Channel

Channel
Islands

FRANCE

St. Nazaire

Destroyer
Patrol Line

OUTWARD ROUTE

PLANNED
RETURN ROUTE

Rendezvous
Points

A

B

C

D

T

E

Y

Z

N
W E
S

0   50   100 miles

directly observed Ryder's ruse her captain nevertheless reported the convoy's heading as 'course west'. The five German destroyers had headed out on their normal patrol run on the strength of that communication and fortunately never sighted Ryder's flotilla. At 11.00 a.m., with the situation appearing normal, the fleet resumed its journey. The convoy and the mission were saved: for the time being.

A little after 11.35 a.m. the crews of two French trawlers which had marked the outer limits of a cluster of fishing boats were taken on board the destroyers and their boats sunk as a precaution against the possibility of their carrying signal equipment.

On reaching Point 'D', Ryder signalled a course south of east that he hoped would lull hostile observers into the false assumption that he was of heading for La Rochelle.

At 8.00 p.m. in the gathering gloom, the convoy halted at position 'E'. This was quite probably the point of no return. They were now only 65 miles and just a few hours from charging straight into the mouth of the River Loire and into the teeth of the German guns on the final run into St. Nazaire, a port the Germans felt was nigh on impregnable. Proof of this had come that same day, even as the Chariot force was sailing towards its destiny. Admiral Karl Dönitz, Commander in Chief of Germany's U-Boat forces, had chosen that day of all days to tour the submarine pens at St. Nazaire, escorted by *Kapitänleutnant* Herbert Sohler, commander of the 7th U-Boat Flotilla. Dönitz had enquired what Sohler had in mind to do should the British decide to mount an attack. Sohler assured his Admiral that plans had been made but no-one in St. Nazaire on 27th March seriously expected a raid from the sea. *'That is considered here to be highly improbable'* remarked Sohler with more than a hint of complacency. Perhaps with the words of Hitler's Directive No. 40 on 'Command Organisation on the Coasts' - an almost prophetic warning of imminent British attacks, issued just four days earlier - still ringing in his ears the Admiral's response was a terse, *'I should not be too sure'*.

If only he had known. If only he could have seen the force now begin to assume its attack formation as MGB 314 took on its naval and military HQ staff of Ryder and Newman and loosed

Admiral Karl Dönitz, Commander in Chief of Germany's U-Boat forces.

Right: *Kapitänleutnant Herbert Sohler, commander of the 7th U-Boat Flottilla.*

Admiral Karl Dönitz opening the U-boat pens at St. Nazaire, June 1941. Dönitz was to revisit St. Nazaire in 1942 whilst the Chariot attack force was steaming towards the Loire estuary.

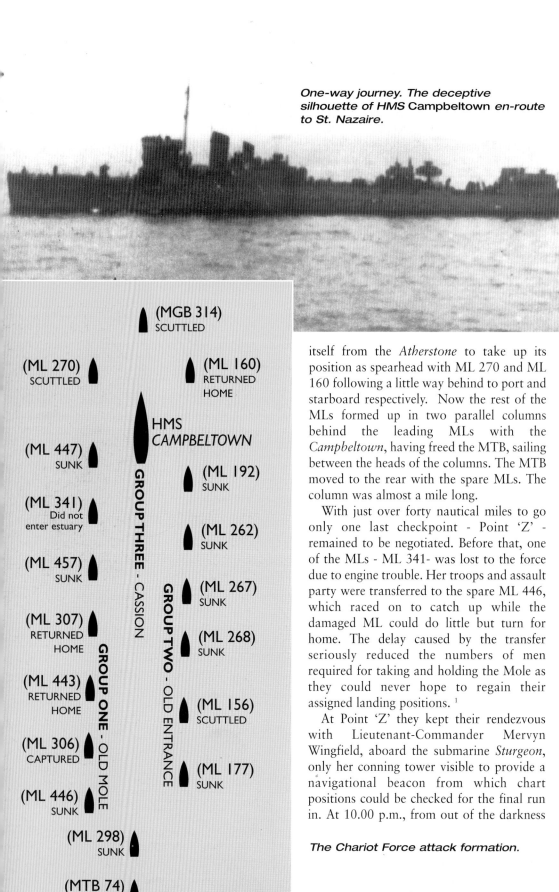

One-way journey. The deceptive silhouette of HMS Campbeltown *en-route to St. Nazaire.*

(MGB 314) SCUTTLED

(ML 270) SCUTTLED

(ML 160) RETURNED HOME

HMS CAMPBELTOWN

(ML 447) SUNK

(ML 192) SUNK

(ML 341) Did not enter estuary

(ML 262) SUNK

(ML 457) SUNK

(ML 267) SUNK

GROUP THREE - CASSION

(ML 307) RETURNED HOME

GROUP TWO - OLD ENTRANCE

(ML 268) SUNK

(ML 443) RETURNED HOME

GROUP ONE - OLD MOLE

(ML 156) SCUTTLED

(ML 306) CAPTURED

(ML 177) SUNK

(ML 446) SUNK

(ML 298) SUNK

(MTB 74) SUNK

itself from the *Atherstone* to take up its position as spearhead with ML 270 and ML 160 following a little way behind to port and starboard respectively. Now the rest of the MLs formed up in two parallel columns behind the leading MLs with the *Campbeltown*, having freed the MTB, sailing between the heads of the columns. The MTB moved to the rear with the spare MLs. The column was almost a mile long.

With just over forty nautical miles to go only one last checkpoint - Point 'Z' - remained to be negotiated. Before that, one of the MLs - ML 341- was lost to the force due to engine trouble. Her troops and assault party were transferred to the spare ML 446, which raced on to catch up while the damaged ML could do little but turn for home. The delay caused by the transfer seriously reduced the numbers of men required for taking and holding the Mole as they could never hope to regain their assigned landing positions. [1]

At Point 'Z' they kept their rendezvous with Lieutenant-Commander Mervyn Wingfield, aboard the submarine *Sturgeon*, only her conning tower visible to provide a navigational beacon from which chart positions could be checked for the final run in. At 10.00 p.m., from out of the darkness

The Chariot Force attack formation.

Sturgeon's light began to flash intermittently, signalling the letter 'M'. It was dead ahead and dead on time.

Now *Tynedale* and *Atherstone* broke away to establish a patrol-line across the course the surviving MLs were expected to follow as they returned to rendezvous position 'T' on their way home after the attack. Denuded of the reassuring presence and firepower of the destroyers' guns the rest of the fleet now felt uncomfortably vulnerable.

By 11.00 p.m. the rendezvous with *Sturgeon* had, like its extinguished beacon, become a faded memory. With muscles tightening and mouths drying the men began mental rehearsals as they ran through their attack positions and responsibilities. This was it.

'A CHEERY VOICE'

By Sir Ronald Swayne MC Ex - Lieutenant, Herefordshire Regiment and I Commando

So we set sail, not for St. Nazaire but for Spain, right down through the Bay of Biscay - lovely weather. We were a submarine sweep with the destroyers and the MLs... One always felt that there might be a German aeroplane in the clouds looking at us. One had a sort of feeling of some hidden eye watching us, either from a periscope or through the clouds but I don't think they knew we there until right at the end.

We went quite far down south of the Loire entrance and came back again on our sort of north-east to make the rendezvous with the submarine which was the beacon the column had to contact. From that point we were on our own and the destroyers remained behind. We navigated behind *Campbeltown* up the estuary and up the river and that all worked absolutely perfectly. There was a navigator called Lieutenant Green, he was a specialist navigator who got us to the submarine and my ML [306] passed actually just behind it. It was as close as that - and I heard a cheery voice. And then we were on our way up the river.

Sir Ronald Swayne M.C., *The Commandos* IWM Sound Archive 10231/3 (1988)

JELLYFISH LIGHT THE WAY TO ST. NAZAIRE

By Ralph Batteson. Ex-Ordinary Seaman RN - Aft Gunner ML 306

We felt excited and we knew something was going to happen but only the officers and people in the know knew we were going into St. Nazaire. We didn't know it was St. Nazaire until we were taken prisoner! I don't think I ever got the chance to get nervous there was always something to do. I'm one of those types of chaps who can keep my cool normally. I was never afraid, although there were plenty of things going on around me. Just before we got into St. Nazaire we bumped into a lot of French fishing boats and the escort destroyers dashed off to see what was happening. They thought that the fishing boats could have had Germans on board with radios to warn that we were coming. They got two fishing boats separated from the others and found out that there was no means of communication with the shore. But because these two had seen more of us than anybody else - all the motor launches and the MTB - and they must have known we were quite close to the French coast, they could have sent signals back to the shore and warned the Germans about us. So they sunk these two boats and the French crew were quite happy to go with us, in fact they were quite happy to leave German occupied France.

The night we were going into St. Nazaire the sea was alight with this phosphorescence coming off the jellyfish. I've never seen so many. We were cutting through them. There were millions of them.

IWM Sound Archive 22668

THE GERMANS

U p until the mid 1850s, the port of St. Nazaire, resting on the north bank of the River Loire, a full six miles upstream from its gaping mouth, had been overshadowed by the much larger and more important trading port of Nantes, a further thirty five miles up the swiftly flowing artery. But the advent of the age of steam, and the corresponding increase in the size of steam-powered ships, signalled the end of Nantes's command of the Loire as the river's currents and bewildering tangle of mud flats and shoals rendered it impassable for these larger modern vessels. Undaunted the French sought to develop the erstwhile fishing village of St. Nazaire, much closer to the Biscay Coast and providing direct access to the Atlantic, as the premier port on the Loire. New sheltered docks, port installations and shipbuilding facilities were planned and eventually constructed, one of the last being the *Normandie* dry dock - the key target of the Chariot raiders - completed in the 1920s.[1]

GERMAN NAVAL TROOPS DEFENDING ST. NAZAIRE
28TH MARCH 1942

SEE KOMMANDANT LOIRE

Kapitän zur See Zuckschwerdt
Officer Commanding German Naval Troops of Port of St. Nazaire
HQ - La Baule

280th Naval Artillery Battalion

OC - *Korvettenkapitän* Edo Dieckmann
HQ - Chémoulin Point

22nd Naval Flak Brigade

OC - *Kapitän zur See* C.C. Mecke
HQ - St. Marc

St Nazaire Harbour Defences

Harbour Commader (*Hafenkommandant*) *Korvettenkapitän* Kellermann
HQ - Boulevard President Wilson (On leave at the time of the raid)

703rd Battalion

OC - *Korvettenkapitän* Thiessen
HQ - Villès-Martin

705th Battalion

OC - *Korvettenkapitän* Koch

809th Battalion

OC - *Korvettenkapitän* Burhenne
HQ - South bank of Loire between Pionte de Mindin and Le Pointeau

The Germans came to St. Nazaire in June 1940. Turning their attentions to the rest of France after the operational success of their *Fall Gelb* and the allied evacuations from Dunkirk in the north, the Germans swept all before them as they drove south, despite the best efforts of the French and British to stem the tide. Hurried evacuations from Normandy and a number of the Biscay ports followed. Between 15th - 19th June 57,235 British and allied troops were evacuated from St. Nazaire - Captain Bob Montgomery, who later used his first hand knowledge of the port to develop schemes for the destruction of many of the key targets included in the 'Chariot' plan with Captain Bill Pritchard - was one of them. [2]

For the Germans tasked with developing the coastal defences around St. Nazaire after its occupation, its position and natural barriers could not have been more providential when planning to confound a sea-borne operation. The port was, after all, still six miles upstream from the mouth of a fast flowing river and its approaches across the treacherous mud flats and extensive shoals were hazardous to say the least. Only one narrow passageway - the Charpentier Channel - was deep enough for larger ships to navigate with any degree of safety. Running for some nine nautical miles from the mouth of the Loire off the Pointe de Chamoulin in a long, slow northerly arc, the channel almost caressed the northern bank at the Pointe de l'Eve on its way into the port. Its proximity to the coast was a Godsend for the Germans who assiduously constructed their own defences - on both banks - to add weight to these not inconsiderable natural barriers to allied attack. Not surprisingly the bulk of the German guns, under the overall command of *See Kommandant* Loire, *Kapitän zur See* Zuckschwerdt were arrayed along the northern bank to dominate and screen the channel. Any force which tried to negotiate the approaches to and then enter the Charpentier Channel, would not only have to steer clear of the shallows but would have to run the lengthy gauntlet of a fearsome array of guns bearing down on them from both north and south banks, many at fairly close quarters. Including the two, 240mm railway guns of the Battery Batz, way out to the west near La Pouliguen and covering the approach off the Pointe de Penchateau, there were six, fixed heavy coastal batteries of the 280th Naval Artillery Battalion under the command of *Korvettenkapitän* Edo Dieckmann. Apart from the 240mm guns, Dieckmann's batteries each consisted of four guns ranging from 75-170mm. No less than three of those batteries were clustered on the north bank covering the Charpentier Channel. Nearer the port itself three battalions of the 22nd Naval Flak Brigade under *Kapitän zur See* C.C. Mecke had forty-three guns, ranging from 20 - 40mm able to be used in a dual role against both air and surface raiders, mounted on top of concrete bunkers, flak towers and the roofs of the nine U-Boat pens then constructed. In addition there were three, heavy anti-aircraft batteries, each of four 75mm guns, which admittedly, could only engage air targets and the weaponry was augmented by four, powerful 'five foot' searchlights and numerous smaller ones. To make matters worse the 996-ton *Sperrbrecher* 137, a 'barrage breaker' bristling with 20mm Oerlikons and a fearsome '88', and with a reputation for accuracy and destructive force, was moored in the estuary just off the eastern jetty of the Avant Port. In the harbour itself were men of the guard companies, technicians of Numbers 2 and 4 Works Companies and U-Boat maintenance staff - with orders to defend, or in the worst case, destroy their boats if necessary - along with the not insubstantial

A. 20 mm-Flakvierling 38. B. 37 mm Flak 18. C. 88 mm Flak 18

numbers of men crewing the various vessels moored in the harbour of St. Nazaire at the time. Amongst others these included the four harbour defence boats, ten minesweepers and five tugs. All these men could use the available weaponry on board their vessels or act as infantry to plug gaps and hold the line until more experienced and better-equipped troops could be rushed into action. Not too far away inland was a brigade of soldiers of the 333rd Infantry Division which could and doubtless would, be mobilised to help repel an incursion. By anyone's standards the defences of St. Nazaire were formidable. In all, there were estimated to be some 6,000 German troops and attached personnel defending St. Nazaire, 1,000 of them arrayed along the banks of the Loire with the rest in and around the docks complex.[3]

Little wonder then that the German authorities felt secure in their assessment that St. Nazaire was a 'low risk' target. Their reckoning did not take into account the Chariot Force. Now sailing towards them on board the *Campbeltown* and the MLs were the 611 men - 345 sailors, 166 from the fighting parties of No. 2 Commando, 91 from the demolition teams of the combined Commandos, a four-man medical team, three liaison officers and two gentleman of the press - which constituted the total manpower of the raiding force. Already heavily outgunned and outnumbered in terms of manpower, it would be a fortunate vessel indeed that would survive the six-mile odyssey along such a shooting gallery and the force would have to use every trick of deception up its sleeve to buy precious minutes to deliver it as near to its target as possible. Little wonder that when news of the raid finally broke, it evoked echoes and images of the ill-fated Light Brigade, thundering into the jaws of the 'Valley of Death' at Balaclava during the Crimean War.

[1] Winston G. Ramsey, The Raid on Saint Nazaire, *After the Battle*, 59, (1988)

[2] See James G. Dorrian *Storming St. Nazaire* (Barnsley: Leo Cooper, 2001) pp. 16-17

[3] C.E. Lucas Phillips, *The Greatest Raid of All* (London: Pan, 2000) pp. 104-105

ST NAZAIRE
OPERATION CHARIOT

THE ATTACK RUN

For at least one German commander on the ground, the behaviour of the British bombers, which had first appeared over St. Nazaire at around 11.30 p.m. on 27th March, was peculiar to say the least. Instead of conforming to an established pattern of pounding numerous targets in and around the docks, the successive waves of sixty-two Armstrong Whitworth Whitleys and Wellingtons appeared to circle aimlessly above the cloud ceiling, which had dropped to below 6,000 feet.

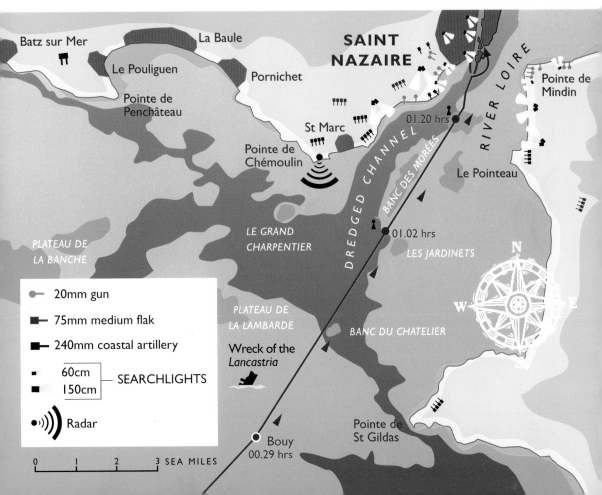

Batz sur Mer
La Baule
SAINT NAZAIRE
RIVER LOIRE
Le Pouliguen
Pointe de Mindìn
Pornichet
Pointe de Penchâteau
St Marc
01.20 hrs
Pointe de Chémoulin
DREDGED CHANNEL
BANC DES MORÉES
Le Pointeau
PLATEAU DE LA BANCHE
LE GRAND CHARPENTIER
01.02 hrs
LES JARDINETS

N

PLATEAU DE LA LAMBARDE
BANC DU CHATELIER

W   E

Wreck of the *Lancastria*

S

Pointe de St Gildas

Bouy
00.29 hrs

Legend:
- ●— 20mm gun
- ■— 75mm medium flak
- ■— 240mm coastal artillery
- ■ 60cm — SEARCHLIGHTS
- ■ 150cm
- ●·))) Radar

0   1   2   3 SEA MILES

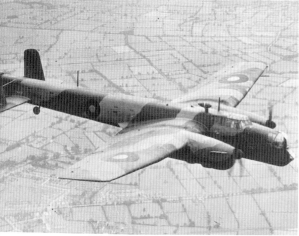 

Above left to right: Whitley Whitworth and the Wellington Bomber. These were used to divert the Germans' attention whilst the Chariot Force made its way up the Loire estuary.

From his HQ at St. Marc, *Kapitän zur See* Mecke had ordered his 22nd Flak Brigade to put up a murderous fire to see off the British planes but gradually, as the 'raid' developed, so his suspicions had been aroused. These blundering bombers, dropping only one bomb per plane per bombing run, and even then apparently targeting only the *Normandie* dock and the Penhoët Basin, were not simply engaged on a 'routine' bombing raid to destroy the dock installations. Something else was going on. Perhaps they were a preliminary to some other, more violent scheme? So sure was he that he voiced his fears to one of his staff officers. His comment, *'Some devilry is afoot'*, was almost Shakespearean in its delivery. At midnight he formalised his fears in a signal to all command posts of the *Wehrmacht*: *'The conduct of the enemy aircraft is inexplicable and indicates suspicion of parachute landings'.*[1] He was right to be wary of course, but the real threat was not to be from the air.

'Some devilry is afoot'

The bombers were indeed part of the overall plan to divert German attention away from the real business of the night but the very fact that their objectives had been limited in order to spare the lives of the civilian population had only served to heighten German suspicions. It was not the fault of the bomber crews. Hamstrung by operational orders, they were completely oblivious of the grand design. All they knew was that they had been forbidden to drop their bombs below 6,000 feet and that their targets had been severely restricted.

Arriving off the mouth of the Loire just after midnight on the 28th the Chariot Force adopted its attack formation and began its run in towards the shoals and shallows. As Major Bill Copland chaired a final briefing of his officers in the *Campbeltown*'s wardroom, the eyes of the rest of the members of the Chariot force were drawn to the flickering canopy of flak and searchlight beams playing in the sky almost dead ahead as the British bombers bumbled around for a little while longer then finally turned for home. Then the sky grew dark again. The air raid, originally planned in three phases to last until 4.00 a.m., was effectively over in little more than forty minutes, with many of the planes beginning to make their long journey home with their bomb racks still groaning under the weight of a full load. [2]

At 00.45 the *Campbeltown*, flying the German flag, scraped the bottom lightly near the Banc du Chatelier and did so again some ten minutes later. These alarums aside, the flotilla pressed on unimpeded and swept past a German patrol boat that spotted them but fortunately lacked a radio to relay a signal ashore. Luck continued to smile on the brave as a confirmed sighting, reported to the HQ of the absent Harbour Commander by none other than *Korvettenkapitän* Burhenne, the commander of Mecke's 809th Flak Battalion, was dismissed with contempt. At 1.20 a.m., MGB 314, with Ryder and Newman on board, passed the Les Morées tower. Just behind them, the *Campbeltown* was now less than two miles and just fifteen minutes from target - the *Normandie* Dock.

It was the five-foot searchlight, 'Blue 1', just inland from the Villès-Martin HQ of *Korvettenkapitän* Thiessen, commanding the 703rd Flak Battalion, which, two minutes later, first illuminated the threat now surging towards St. Nazaire. Others quickly followed, flooding the Charpentier Channel with intense white light, fixing the fleet in their brilliant glare. Two 20mm guns barked out warning salvoes whilst signal lamps from up ahead and beyond the starboard bow blinked enquiringly in challenge. Pretending to be a German convoy returning to port, Leading Signalman Pike, with Ryder on board MGB 314, replied using genuine German call signs provided by intelligence. The pre-prepared, long-winded message confused the Germans sufficiently to elicit a slight pause in their firing and bought four priceless minutes - precious moments at this stage in the attack run. But the bluffing couldn't last. Even as Ryder used the last of his ruses - firing a flare signal from a Very pistol in the colour used by the Germans to respond to a challenge, which ironically ditched in the water rather than soaring into the night sky - the very air seemed to be rent asunder as the German guns opened fire in earnest. It was 1.28 a.m. The game was finally up.

Now the Germans really showed their hand and the punishment for Ryder's 'effrontery' was swift and destructive as the flotilla was raked by fire from dozens of guns ranged on the north and south banks of the estuary and from the port itself. Holding his nerve Beattie first ordered the *Campbeltown* to increase speed to eighteen knots and then ordered, 'Hoist battle ensigns.' With no need now for pretence, the German colours were taken down - a strip of it was torn off in the midst of the maelstrom and handed to Captain Roy to carry in his tunic by his batman Gunner Milne - and the White Ensign run up as Beattie guided her through the storm. Strung out for more than a mile behind, the rest of the MLs now broke out their White Ensigns too, a sight which swelled the hearts of both sailors and soldiers. Ahead of, and bigger than them all, bathed in the harsh brilliance of numerous searchlights, the elderly *Campbeltown* drew the worst of the German response. Her hull became a quivering mass of flame and sparks as hundreds of direct hits rippled along her flanks.

Beattie had held his fire for long enough and now rang his signal bell. At last the fleet could reply. *Campbeltown*'s Oerlikons were the first to respond, soon followed by the forward 12-pounder which, responding to the full-throated command, 'Let her go' bellowed out by Major Copland, burst into life along with the forward 3-inch mortars. Now the MLs followed suit and both soldier and sailor alike peppered the hostile shores with Oerlikon, Hotchkiss and Bren gun fire, while Able Seaman Bill Savage aboard MGB 314 handled his pom-pom with skill and daring. Those who witnessed it and survived would never forget what Lance Sergeant Don Randall later described as a 'satanic son et lumière' spectacular. [3]

'In a moment upwards of a hundred guns and innumerable small arms were firing, within this small area, nearly all of them rapid firing pieces, their orange flashes stabbing the cold, white glare of the searchlights. Across this great pool of light, into which every lamp that the Germans possessed was now concentrating its shaft, there shot in all directions vivid streams of red, green and yellow tracer. They criss-crossed like lighted shuttles on some infernal loom, duplicated by their darting images on the still water. As orchestra to this dazzling and menacing spectacle there could be heard, above the drumroll of machine-gun and rifle, the prolonged bursts of Oerlikons, the repetitive thud of Bofors, and the sharper cracks of Dieckmann's heavier coast defence guns - 75mm, 150mm 170mm.' [4]

> **'In a moment, upwards of a hundred guns and innumerable small arms were firing...'**

Ahead of the *Campbeltown*, MGB 314 and the Fairmiles under the command of Boyd and Irwin, traded shot for shot with the German guns ashore. Boyd's ML 160 engaged and damaged the shoreline batteries to the east of the dock which could enfilade the destroyer's starboard side when she finally struck home: Irwin's ML 270 meanwhile took on the searchlights now illuminating *Campbeltown*'s bridge and armoured wheelhouse. Although restricted to short-range weapons, their fire was so effective that the German fusillade slackened after three or four minutes but the reprieve was merely temporary. They soon found the range again and the fleet began to take casualties.

Lying, cheek by jowl out on the *Campbeltown*'s open decks, many of the commandos, men such as Lieutenant Stuart Chant, Lance-Sergeant Dai Davis and Fusilier Bill Mattison, were hit by metal fragments from shells or the ship's superstructure. At least they were protected to a certain extent by the specially erected thin, steel screens and fared better than many sailors who, with less protection, were killed on the decks. Trailing in *Campbeltown*'s wake, several of the petrol fuelled Fairmiles towards the rear of the two attack columns burst into flames as shells ruptured their vulnerable fuel tanks, whilst others spun from their stations out of control and out of the line as flimsy wooden hulls were smashed to matchwood. Even so, the British gunners continued to respond with venom. Up ahead the MGB passed close to the *Sperrbrecher* 137 which Able Seaman Savage promptly 'plastered' with his pom-pom, neutralising the threat from its fearsome 88mm. Beattie, now operating from the armoured wheelhouse having vacated the exposed bridge, drove the *Campbeltown* on towards the marker of the lighthouse at the end of the Old Mole, now so kindly illuminated by German searchlights. Ever onward now, her speed approaching twenty knots as she raged through a blizzard

An artist's impression by Commander Ryder, showing the moment Campbeltown *hit the caisson. Ryder's MGB is pictured on the right along with the MLs to the left, heading towards the Old Entrance. In the background are the U-Boat pens and pumping station.*

of red and green tracer, her Oerlikons spitting fire as first she snagged and then ripped through the anti-torpedo nets. Nothing now it seemed could stop her. With her unwounded commandos poised to storm ashore, Beattie called out one final adjustment to flare her stern to starboard and then clung on for dear life like everyone else around him in the wheelhouse. Seconds later *Campbeltown*'s bows crashed dead centre into the massive outer caisson. With a terrible grinding of metal on metal, her hull buckled like tin foil against the caisson as her momentum forced her superstructure further forward. She came to rest at last, protruding some 35 feet over the empty lock; her fo'c'sle perched up and over the caisson - a perfect platform from which her commando parties could disembark. It was 1.34 a.m. As the shuddering ceased Beattie glanced over at Bob Montgomery and, in what must be one of, if not the understatement of the entire Second World War, remarked '*Well, there we are.*' Then he glanced at his watch, '*Four minutes late*' he added! [5]

'**Well there we are... four minutes late.**'

The *Campbeltown*'s one-way ticket had been used to good effect. Beattie's 'delivery' of his 'floating bomb' had been spectacularly successful. His vessel had come to rest with her explosive charge only five feet away from the lock gate. But

Another sketch by Commander Ryder shows the Campbeltown *embedded in the caisson, her cargo of heavily armed Commandos would have by now spilled over the sides and into the fighting. Meanwhile, the motor torpedo boat speeds towards the lock gates. Ryder would have been aboard MGB 314, pictured on the left at the eastern entrance.*

A ticking bomb. The Campbeltown *at daybreak showing the devastating consequences of the collision. The worst was yet to come, a deadly cargo of explosives was ticking away deep inside her bows. Her service as a destroyer was over, her final duty yet to be fulfilled.*

she was no longer a ship. At the point of impact she had metamorphosed almost instantly into an armed and extremely dangerous weapon; an unwelcome Trojan Horse, astride one of Nazi Germany's most prized maritime assets in occupied France, counting down the seconds to its destruction.

'COME IN NO. 7, YOUR TIME IS UP'

By Dr. David Paton - ex-Captain RAMC & No. 2 Commando, Aboard ML 307

I went forward and found two of my chaps changing their uniforms from trousers to kilts. They explained that as they were probably going to die they preferred to die in kilts. Darkness everywhere now and only the phosphorescence of the sea to see by. Full speed ahead and we seemed to be in the estuary with even blacker black on both sides. The engine throbbing was all that could be heard. Then a signal light ashore flashed a message to us, in German. The *Campbeltown* replied, in German. We steamed on, faster and faster now. A searchlight beam fell on the *Campbeltown* and she replied by unfurling a simply gigantic Nazi Swastika. Seconds went by, we were getting nearer. Then a German gun fired once and we made no reply. Meanwhile we had passed the *Campbeltown* which had stuck on a mud flat. Then it passed us again and we passed it as it stuck once more. Then all hell broke loose. Searchlights by the dozen illuminated us from both sides and we became shooting targets for a huge variety of guns. At first I took cover behind a depth charge on the deck, but a bit of that went whizzing past my ear so I stood up. The corporal next to me took over the rear Oerlikon gun and began firing at the lights till the Skipper [Lieutenant Norman Wallis RANVR] came back and said not to fire any more for we wanted some ammunition to get home with. I couldn't see anything of the big shells which must have been falling but the air was thick with tracer shells coming from all directions rather like cricket balls. You could see them coming and jump out of the way, or jump up in the air for the same reason. I turned round to see how the boat behind was getting on and found it had just disappeared bearing the Sergeant Major and the Colt he had promised me if we both got back. I envied Commander Beattie in the *Campbeltown*, he at least was in an armoured tower while we were in wooden boats with no protection at all. Ahead I saw the *Campbeltown* just about to move into the dock gates and here we were at the Old Mole, for all the world like a boating lake when your time is up, 'Come in No.7!'

'JUST LIKE A FIREWORK DISPLAY'

By Ralph Batteson. Ex-Ordinary Seaman RN - Aft Gunner ML 306

Everything was kept quiet ... because of fears about the Germans getting to know. It was bad enough going in there unbeknown to the Germans because it was such a good defensive harbour and if they'd have known we were coming they would have wiped us off the face of the earth before we even got into St. Nazaire. We had to have some kind of a game to play with them and it worked successfully. We had a signalman on Commander Ryder's gunboat. He sent a signal out in German - we'd cracked the German code for that day or two - and he sent messages to the shore to tell them we were a German naval patrol that had been in action with the enemy and that we had wounded men on board and we wanted to bring them in to St. Nazaire for treatment. It went on for quite a while until we got right up so that the *Campbeltown* could make its last bit of a dash to crash the lock gates. With the bombers coming over and dropping one or two and the ack-ack firing at them, there was something going off and as we gradually closed up to St. Nazaire itself, there were two lines of motor launches and the *Campbeltown* was leading them. I was strapped into my Oerlikon. Our boat was near the rear of the port column, not right at the end but pretty close to it....but as soon as the Germans opened up and they said 'open fire' well, it was like all hell let loose. Lieutenant Landy was pointing, giving me directions; telling me where to fire. But you had enough guns firing at you to know where to fire in any case - searchlights as well. They were one of the biggest problems. The Germans were switching them off when we got a line of fire on to them and then as soon as we'd swung off them they'd switch them back on and they'd be as deadly as ever. After we'd been firing at one or two of these searchlights to try and stop them picking out the boats, Landy said, "Hang on. Don't swing away from that setting, mark it in your mind and keep it there and then as soon as they light up again let 'em have it." Well we did that on two or three occasions and we must have blown some of them up. You can't be certain. It's just like a firework display and you're in the middle of it. They're firing at you and you're firing at them. You don't want to see anything like that again I'll tell you. It was enough just the once!

IWM Sound Archive 22668

LIT UP LIKE NEW BRIGHTON

By Harold Roberts. Ex – Lance Corporal, 2nd Battalion Liverpool Scottish and 5 Troop, No.2 Commando.

We eventually went to Falmouth to get on the *Campbeltown*, which was an old American destroyer converted to have the appearance of a German ship. There were twenty-four depth charges linked together in the bow and concreted in. Fuses were laid to the explosives to go up at a certain time. The fuses were only put on later. We were billeted on top of that concrete!! The *Campbeltown* was stripped of all the heavy guns because when they were going into St. Nazaire, they had to go through these sand banks and they could only get through those on what they called the neap tide, the highest tide we could get. So we had to go in on a neap tide and we were scraping the bottom then. All the guns had been taken off. We had a 12-pounder on the front.

We knew we were going somewhere but we didn't know where. We weren't allowed into the town, they kept us out of sight. We didn't have anyone clustered on the bow or the decks. Nobody knew we were going on to St. Nazaire. We were trying to guess where we were going while we were getting to know each other - getting to know the naval people. They had a naval commander of the destroyer [Commander Beattie] and an overall commander called Ryder. Then we had our Colonel - Charles Newman - over the army commando lads. He was a great fellow, very approachable, he was a good mixer with his troops if they had a complaint or anything like that. He had a good second in command, Major Bill Copland. They were both approachable and always put the servicemen before themselves, they were always the last. If we were on a route march the men sat down to a meal before they did, "everything all right?" "yes sir" and they went on their way. They made sure that you knew everything that was going on. When we got to know we were going to St. Nazaire, on the way there we saw these maps of where we were going.

Captain Donald Roy was our Captain. He was in charge of 5 Troop. He was good. He was a Scots fella' and he was a good bloke – a big, six-footer. When we went on schemes he was always in the front - "You've got to keep up with me, not me keep up with you", sort of thing. We also had an RSM called Alan Moss. He was a good bloke, came up out of the ranks - just like us but soldiering was in him. George Haines was a senior sergeant. They were all good blokes. We'd been living and working together, so we'd all got to know each other.

We had to travel up the estuary of the River Loire for about six miles but before we got to the estuary there were these sandbanks. We had to get over them and we were scraping the bottom – we were wondering, are we going to get stuck, are we going to get stuck? - but we gradually inched our way through. Then we started going up and we were getting signals from either side, from both banks where all the Germans were. As we were going in we were flying a Swastika flag. I was on the deck, on the left hand side in the middle. They had an 18-inch high steel plate and you could crouch down behind it in your positions. Then you were going up the river estuary and you were getting these signals. The biggest thing was surprise or we'd have been blown out of the water. Then a searchlight would come on....and then another and then the Germans fired a shot. We only had Oerlikon guns after the heavy guns had been taken off - a good gun, a repeater, but only light stuff. Then another searchlight came on and we were firing to try and put the searchlights out. I always used to say I thought they were drunk – the Germans, we should have been blown out of the water otherwise. They had heavy stuff both sides of the estuary, they had these big guns and they were after the

The Commander of 5 Troop, Captain Donald Roy DSO.

destroyer. That was the biggest ship. That was leading the MLs in. But they didn't stop her, going full belt. They threw all their searchlights on then and it was like bloody New Brighton, just like daylight. We were lying flat out with our Bren guns …but our fire was only spasmodic. We just rode the gauntlet and hit the dock gate at about twenty knots. She had a reinforced bow so she hit it and she rode it. He [Beattie] embedded her in the gate but he went up. We weren't thrown about much on deck, so as soon as we hit the caisson we went down the side of the destroyer using bamboo ladders and then we were off, making for these guns on top of some warehouses.

IWM Sound Archive 22671 (2002)

[1] C.E. Lucas Phillips, *op.cit.* p. 129.

[2] Two Whitley bombers of 51 Squadron that took part in the raid became casualties that night, one ditching in the channel off Portsmouth and another crashing into the hills above Ilkley in Yorkshire at 5.15 a.m. See James G. Dorrian, *op.cit.* p. 124.

[3] *Ibid*, p.135.

[4] C.E. Lucas Phillips, *op.cit.* p. 135.

[5] *Ibid*, p.141. See also James G. Dorrian, *op.cit.* p. 138. Dorrian records that Sam Beattie's taciturn response was to announce, 'OK, we seem to be there', before he looked at his watch.

THE WEAPONS

T**he St. Nazaire Commandos went into action with a variety of weapons, some of which have almost become recognised as essential 'tools' of the Commando trade. Storming into St. Nazaire in parties designated, 'assault', 'protection' and 'demolition', the Commandos had to achieve their tasks with whatever weaponry and reserves of ammuntion they could carry with them.**

Apart from the guns of the MLs they could not rely on any other form of fire support. Thus a fine balance had to be struck between the need to generate and sustain a great volume of firepower with the requirement for mobility and flexibility.

As some of the first Commandos ashore - tasked with neutralising known German strongpoints and securing the bridgehead - the men of the assault parties were heavily armed and carried weapons which were able to produce a great volume of easily directed fire. Similarly, the parties designated as 'protection' for the lightly armed demolition parties, burdened with rucksacks full of explosive charges, had to be well armed.

One of the most effective close support weapons carried into St. Nazaire was the Bren MkI light machine-gun. Based on a Czechoslovak Arms Factory Ltd. design from the 1920s, the Bren ('Br' from Brno, the location of the factory in Czechoslovakia and 'En' from Enfield) had entered service with the British Army as recently as 1938. Gas operated and with a barrrel which could be changed at the flick of a catch, it drew its ammunition from a distinctive curved, overhead box magazine. It became one of the best loved British weapons of World War Two. A good deal of its appeal was its portability; either fired from the hip or using its integral bipod. It was very accurate and extremely effective and was used both on land and from the decks of the *Campbeltown* and the MLs during the attack run up the Loire.

Perhaps the weapon most closely associated with the Commandos is the Thompson Model 1928 A1 submachine-gun. Manufactured in the United States the 'Tommy gun', with its 50 round drum magazine, had become almost the weapon of choice for US gangsters. Using the standard US service .45 automatic pistol cartridge - the same ammunition used in the Colt .45s carried by the St. Nazaire Commandos - it was, at 10 lbs, rather heavy and ineffective at long range. These drawbacks were more than compensated for by its balance, volume of fire and stopping power at short range. The drum magazine seen in gangster films was rejected by the Commandos in favour of a twenty round box magazine which was less prone to jam, lighter and easier to pack in ammunition pouches.

The fighting knife is another weapon closely associated with Commandos in combat, the most famous of which was the Fairbairn Sykes (FS) fighting knife. The first pattern, produced in collaboration with Wilkinson Sword in 1940, featured an 'S' shaped cross guard and 8 ½ inch blade. The second pattern dropped the 'S' cross guard in order to speed up production. There is little evidence to suggest that the Commandos had much opportunity to use the FS knife during the raid, in fact Lieutenant Ronald Swayne surrendered his FS knife to *Korvettenkapitän* Friedrich Paul after the capture of ML 306. There were also recorded instances of Commandos discarding their fighting knives prior to capture fearing that the Germans might discover them and thus dispense summary justice. Fairbairn and Sykes were also responsible for the development of the Smatchet, a much larger and fearsome double-edged weapon.

'A HANDY WEAPON'

By Harold Roberts. Ex – Lance Corporal, 2nd Battalion Liverpool Scottish and 5 Troop, No.2 Commando.

The Bren gun was quite a good weapon, accurate and not very heavy. We had the Thompson sub-machine gun from America. It had a drum with fifty rounds of .45 ammunition. The Tommy gun was a handy weapon. It wasn't big and it was easy to carry. It was very potent and accurate used in short bursts at twenty-five to thirty yards. The .45 rounds were lethal. It jammed now and again but it was your weapon and you had to look after it. I had to clean it all so it didn't jam. Sometimes you'd be climbing trees or climbing walls and you might bang it, but there was always an armourer to go and see and get it tested. We had 2 and 3-inch mortars. We had specialists on each weapon - you all had your own weapon. I had a Tommy gun and then a Bren Gun and eventually you'd get round them all, but I never got around to a mortar.'

1 BREN MK I LIGHT MACHINE GUN

2 MKIII SHORT MAGAZINE LEE ENFIELD (SMLE)

3 THOMPSON SUB-MACHINE GUN

4 BOYES ANTI-TANK RIFLE

COLT 45 - M1911 A1 **5**

MILLS HAND GRENADE No. 36 M Mk I **6**

KNUCKLE KNIVES **7a**

7b

FAIRBAIRN-SYKES COMMANDO DAGGER **8**

SMATCHET **9**

71

Illustrations by Jon Wilkinson

TECHNICAL SPECIFICATIONS

① BREN MKI LIGHT MACHINE GUN

Calibre: .303 inch • **Weight:** 10.05 kg (22 lb)
Length: 1,156 mm (45.5 inch) • **Barrel length:** 635 mm (25 inch)
Muzzle velocity: 2,440 ft per second
Magazine: 30 round box

② MKIII SHORT MAGAZINE LEE ENFIELD (SMLE)

Calibre: .303 inch • **Weight:** 8 lbs (empty)
Length: 1143mm • **Barrel length:** 2 ft
Muzzle velocity: 2,440 ft per second • **Magazine:** 10 round box
Effective range: 3,000 metres

③ THOMPSON SUB MACHINE GUN

Calibre: .45 inch • **Weight:** 10 lb
Length: (858 mm) 33.75 inch • **Barrel length:** (260 mm) 10.25 inch
Muzzle velocity: 918 ft per second •
Magazine: 20 round box or a 50 and 100 round drum magazine. A 30 round box magazine was introduced in 1942.

④ BOYES ANTI - TANK RIFLE

Calibre: .55 inch • **Weight:** 36 lb
Length: 63.5 inch • **Barrel length:** 36 inch
Muzzle velocity: 390m (2,750ft) per second
Magazine: 5 round box
System of operation: Bolt action

⑤ COLT 45 - M1911A1

Calibre: .45 inch • **Weight:** 3 lb
Length: (219 mm) 8.5 inch • **Barrel length:** (128 mm) 5.03 inch
Muzzle velocity: 252 m (825 ft) per second • **Magazine:** 7 round box

⑥ MILLS HAND GRENADE No. 36 Mk 1

Length: 3.75 inch (95.2 mm) • **Weight:** 1lb 11oz • **Filling:** Baratol • **Delay:** 4 sec

⑦ KNUCKLE KNIVES

7a: Combined knuckle duster and knife BC41 Pattern • **7b:** 'Fanny' knuckle knife

⑧ FAIRBAIRN SYKES COMMANDO DAGGER PATTERN 2

Blade Length: 7 inch • **Weight:** 0.75 lb

⑨ SMATCHET

Length: 17 inch • Nicknamed the 'Roman Sword' and designed by Fairbairn Sykes.

THE LANDINGS

The *Campbeltown's* one-way ticket had expired the moment Beattie had embedded her into the outer caisson but her task was not yet over. Buried deep in her bow were the twenty-four, 400lb depth charges - set to detonate later - and she still had her human cargo of Commandos to disgorge onto the quays to wreak further destruction. The *Campbeltown's* odyssey to St. Nazaire had never been planned as anything other than a one-way trip but as difficult as their tasks were and as daunting as the odds against them appeared, some men believed they could still do the job and get home. Sadly the journey to St. Nazaire was to be, like the *Campbeltown's*, a one-way trip for many of the Commando assault, demolition and protection parties and the sailors aboard the MLs as the battle against ferocious German resistance developed.

The old destroyer had taken a dreadful pounding on the way in and half the men on board had either been killed or had sustained wounds of varying severity by the time she had rammed the outer caisson. In the end, some 40 percent of the remaining Commandos aboard the *Campbeltown* and the MLs – a little over 370 Commandos, seven parties of which came in aboard the destroyer itself - managed to get 'boots on the ground' ashore. They were all destined to fight bitter, bloody and often lonely battles as they struggled to complete their tasks. Some, in the face of overwhelming odds, failed; others triumphed, but their success came at a heavy price indeed.

Such musings on what the future may or may not hold was perhaps not at the forefront of the *Campbeltown's* Commandos' minds in the chaotic minutes immediately following the impact. The German fire had not slackened simply because the destroyer had come to a grinding halt. There was already a gaping hole, two thirds of the way across the foredeck, in the spot where her forward 12-pounder had been just prior to ramming and German shells continued to pummel the ship. Concentrating on their allotted tasks - all targets in the immediate area of the

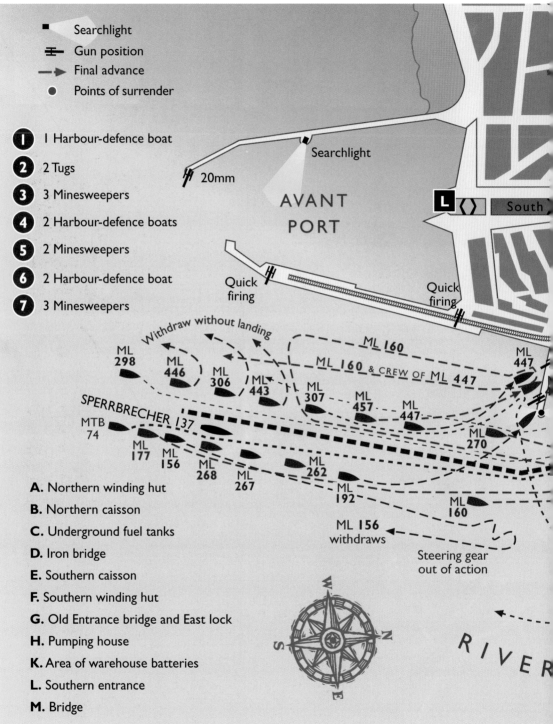

Searchlight

Gun position

Final advance

Points of surrender

1 1 Harbour-defence boat

2 2 Tugs

3 3 Minesweepers

4 2 Harbour-defence boats

5 2 Minesweepers

6 2 Harbour-defence boat

7 3 Minesweepers

Searchlight

20mm

AVANT PORT

L ⟨⟩ South

Quick firing

Quick firing

Withdraw without landing

ML 298

ML 446

ML 306

ML 443

ML 160

ML 160 & CREW OF ML 447

ML 447

ML 307

ML 457

ML 447

ML 270

SPERRBRECHER 137

MTB 74

ML 177

ML 156

ML 268

ML 267

ML 262

ML 192

ML 160

ML 156 withdraws

Steering gear out of action

A. Northern winding hut

B. Northern caisson

C. Underground fuel tanks

D. Iron bridge

E. Southern caisson

F. Southern winding hut

G. Old Entrance bridge and East lock

H. Pumping house

K. Area of warehouse batteries

L. Southern entrance

M. Bridge

RIVER

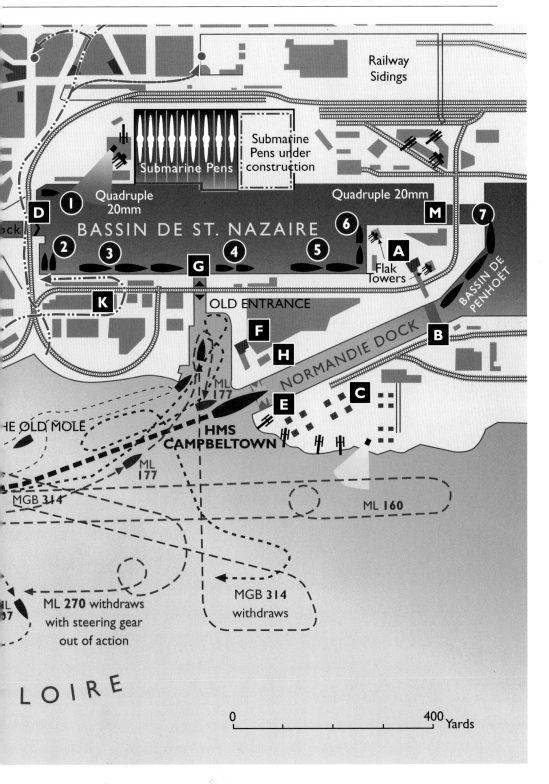

Railway
Sidings

Submarine Pens

Submarine
Pens under
construction

Quadruple
20mm

Quadruple 20mm

D **1**

M **7**

BASSIN DE ST. NAZAIRE **6**

2 **3** **4** **5**

A

Flak
Towers

G

BASSIN DE PENHOËT

K

OLD ENTRANCE

F

H

B

ML
177

E

C

NORMANDIE DOCK

THE OLD MOLE

**HMS
CAMPBELTOWN**

ML
177

MGB 314

ML 160

ML 270 withdraws
with steering gear
out of action

MGB 314
withdraws

L O I R E

0   400 Yards

Normandie dock - the surviving Group 3 Commando parties drew on their weeks of training and swung into action as they prepared to storm ashore, leaving the sacrificial destroyer to her fate and even now settling by the stern as water gushed in through the sea cocks below decks, deliberately opened to scuttle the ship and prevent the Germans moving her before her final performance.

With a cry of 'Roderick off, Roy off', Major Copland urged his Commandos up towards the bow of the ship; galvanising the two assault parties under Captain Donald Roy and Lieutenant Johnny Roderick which now moved, first to the fo'c'sle and then over the side, to drop on the timber roadway that ran along the top of the caisson. The objective of these parties was to block and secure the right and left flanks of the attack on the foreshore to port and starboard after destroying several guns and searchlights in sandbagged emplacements or sited atop buildings. If not eliminated these guns and lights would be free to wreak havoc during the disembarkation of the *Campbeltown*'s demolition and covering parties as they moved off to search out their targets. Swarming over the starboard bow, Roderick's Commandos would first have to engage and destroy the German guns in their path and then block and hold the right, eastern flank against counter attack. At the same time Roy's team, descending from the port bow, would move west, also destroying key gun positions on top of the large pumping station before heading towards Bridge G, which they were to secure and hold, thus maintaining a bridgehead over which the northern demolition parties could make good their escape towards the re-embarkation point at the Old Mole. The neutralization of these two guns in particular was essential as the destruction of the entire pumping station was the objective of Lieutenant Stuart Chant of 2 Commando and the four sergeants of his demolition party.

> 'When we hit, the *Campbeltown* rode much higher up the caisson than we expected and my assault ladder did not reach the dock...'

Clambering down ropes and ladders, with unblackened faces and white blancoed webbing to aid identification, the honour of being the first Commando ashore in the St. Nazaire Raid went to Corporals Woodiwiss and Finch; Tommy gunners from Lieutenant Roderick's party. Leaving the mortally wounded Corporal Donaldson on deck, Woodiwiss, Finch and the rest of Lieutenant Roderick's party successfully destroyed four gun emplacements with 'brutal efficiency' within the space of twenty minutes before moving on to destroy some oil tanks with incendiary charges. Corporal Woodiwiss later revealed his part in the action.

> *'When we hit, the Campbeltown rode much higher up the caisson than we expected and my assault ladder did not reach the dock, so I had to jump down to attack the nearest gun position which was raking us with enfilade fire. Pausing to get my bearings, I saw a potato-masher grenade flying towards me. I fly-kicked this, luckily hitting the handle. It went back where it had come from and sorted out the group who had hurled it. After bitter hand-to-hand fighting, I eliminated the sentries, forced my way into the gun position and sprayed the crew with my Tommy gun. I then wrapped my prepared explosive charge around the breech and destroyed the gun. I*

returned to my assault group and we attacked all the remaining gun positions, then placed our incendiary charges into the oil storage tanks.' [1]

The official German report, compiled after the raid, hinted at certain deficiencies in the state of the defences which allowed the Commandos to get ashore and complete their tasks. The report appears to be at odds with the mood of near complacency prevalent amongst those charged with responsibility for maintaining the St. Nazaire defences just prior to the raid.

Corporal A. F. Woodiwiss, 3 Troop, 2 Commando.

> *'In the dockyard the enemy was able to land unhindered since there were no barbed wire defences on the hard, or on the steps to the jetty and the quay. . . . Other unprotected points were the steps leading to the gun emplacements, searchlight stations and bunker platforms, and important targets such as lock gates, pumping plants, engine installations and U-boat bunkers. There were not enough machine-guns and the hand grenades were for the most part without detonators. The ships' companies and others who had gone to the air-raid shelters when the air-raid warning sounded could not take part in the fighting, although they were right in the battle area, as they were unarmed.'* [2]

The Germans actually mounted more resistance than their report acknowledged and Roderick's team certainly felt the intensity of it as German resistance stiffened in their vicinity. With their mission accomplished, Roderick's party – now down to some ten effective men, having taken several casualties - held on to their positions for another thirty minutes until Roderick eventually ordered a withdrawal at about 2.30 a.m. in response to what his lookout believed to be a green rocket – the pre-arranged signal for withdrawal - sent up from Newman's HQ, now ashore near Bridge G. Sprinting back along the caisson, Roderick's men found that the hulk of the old destroyer effectively barred their way to Bridge G and the Old Mole. Their only option was to climb up, over her and down the other side in order to reach their re-embarkation point. Corporal Woodiwiss was the last to climb aboard.

> *'Lieutenant Roderick ordered our withdrawal. I covered this so that our survivors could re-cross to the ship and regroup. I then climbed the lashed ladder up to the bows and pulled this up to prevent pursuit. A burst of fire indicated a counterattack. A large group of Germans were forming to cross the open area we had just left. Lying abandoned on deck behind the shrapnel shields were Brens with 100-round magazines which had been fired as we sailed up the Loire. I set up three of these behind the shields and began firing each in turn to prevent their advance and forced them to withdraw. The fuses in the six tons of Ammonal below had already been activated, the fire below decks still smouldered and I was lying feet above the charge. I thought discretion was the better part of valour, so decided to leave. I dropped all the spare weapons I could find into the Loire, collected*

A Commando armed with the Bren Gun. Many of the Commando raiders were heavily laden with explosives needed to blow up key objectives. Because of this they had to be lightly armed, making them reliant on the protection parties for cover and suspressive fire whilst placing their charges.

Illustration by Jon Wilkinson.

all the Tommy magazines I could carry, rejoined my section and shared out the ammo'. [3]

By this time Captain Roy's assault party, fourteen strong on paper but already reduced to twelve due to wounds sustained during the attack run, had slithered over the *Campbeltown's* port bow and sprinted through a blizzard of fire from their objective, the 20mm guns atop the pumping station. After putting the German gun crews to flight with well-placed grenades and MG fire, Roy, accompanied by Lance Sergeant Don Randall and Private Johnny Gwynne, climbed up and planted explosives on two of the guns before leading his Commandos at the double towards Bridge G. There, they fought for half an hour with the Germans, now emerging like enraged ants from shelters ashore and on board the minesweepers and harbour defence boats in the harbour basin to man their action stations.

Corporal Harold Roberts, in Roy's party, had gone over the port side of the ship ahead of Private Arthur Ashcroft but Ashcroft, heavily laden with weapons and two haversacks full of grenades, had lost his helmet during a fall into the smouldering crater where *Campbeltown's* forward 12-pounder had so recently stood. Ashcroft went into action with no head protection – a state of affairs which almost proved fatal.

'We were running towards this pump house with the guns on the top. The Germans were up there and they had these ladders and we were getting up there as well. They lobbed a grenade. But the Germans more or less said 'bye bye'. We fired at them and they ran away as far as we knew. The Captain went up and a sergeant went with him and then another three or four lads went with their Tommy guns. We did what we had to do which was to get rid of the guns – they would hold us up. I was down on the ground taking up a defensive position to protect those up above who had gone on to destroy the guns. My position was governed by where the fire was coming from. There were a lot of [German] ships spread about in the St. Nazaire basin and they were firing, perhaps indiscriminately. We were 'dodging the flak', so to speak. So we got rid of the guns on top of the pump house...put

A photograph showing some of the equipment the Commandos were expected to carry into battle. Note that this man is carrying the old American M1917 infantry rifle, sent to Britain as part of the Lend Lease programme.

charges in the barrels and blew them up. I didn't see any dead Germans though. We then had other jobs to do further afield.[4]

With the battle for the bridgehead either side of the *Campbeltown*'s bows beyond the dry dock still raging, Major Copland now ordered the demolition teams and their covering parties off the ship.

His job complete, Commander Beattie had begun to evacuate his crew almost as soon as Major Copland had given the order for his Commandos to disembark. At that point, just minutes after Beattie had rammed *Campbeltown* home and with the Commando carrying MLs of Group 1 (port column) and Group 2 (starboard column) heading for their respective landing points at the Old Mole and the Old Entrance, Colonel Newman and Commander Ryder had still been aboard Lieutenant Dunstan Curtis's MGB 314. The *Sperrbrecher* had suddenly and unexpectedly leapt into life again, adding its considerable firepower to that now being brought to bear on the flimsy MLs downstream. With a strong paternal urge to protect his men on their launches, Ryder was keen to organise its destruction but Newman – with an equally strong urge to organise and lead his Commandos, some of whom were now ashore and engaging the Germans – wanted to be put ashore to establish his HQ. After a brief but heated exchange the military commander won the day. Curtis was ordered in and, in spite of their differences, Newman and Ryder shook hands before Newman scrambled ashore with his party and disappeared into the night. With Newman gone and unsure of the whereabouts of Beattie, Ryder, who was well aware that some of the MLs downstream were already ablaze, then decided to go ashore himself and he ordered Curtis to berth alongside the northern quay of the Old Entrance to the lock. There he took on board as many of *Campbeltown*'s crew – who now dashed for his boat - as he could whilst Rodier's ML 177 - the last launch chronologically in the starboard column yet ironically the only one to have made it relatively unscathed to the Old Entrance to land all its Commandos - did likewise.

> 'We did what we had to do which was to get rid of the guns, they would hold us up.'

There were no easy tasks for any party on the St. Nazaire raid, be they Commando assault, demolition, protection or indeed naval, but the job entrusted to Lieutenant Stuart Chant's small Group 3 team was perhaps one of the most daunting. Chant and his four sergeants were charged with the key task of destroying the impeller pumps and electrical switchgear that controlled the filling and draining of the massive Forme Ecluse dry dock. Even if the *Campbeltown*'s charges failed to detonate and the collision damage to the massive outer caisson was repaired, the destruction of the vital pumps would deny the Germans the use of the dry dock for many months if not years. Now Chant's team were hard on Roy's heels making a beeline for the pumping station.

Chant had been wounded in the knee, arms and fingers during *Campbeltown*'s run in and would go into action with hands badly lacerated by tiny fragments of shrapnel. Sergeant Chamberlain too was wounded. Like Private Ashcroft before – and indeed several others who would follow - Chant had fallen into the smoking hole of the 12-pounder pit and had had to be fished out but the team pressed on

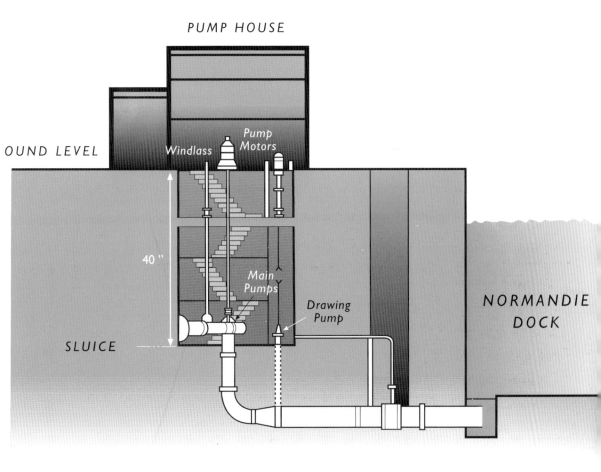

PUMP HOUSE

OUND LEVEL

Windlass

Pump Motors

40 "

Main Pumps

Drawing Pump

SLUICE

NORMANDIE DOCK

A cross section of the pump house. A vital objective, as the pumps were expensive and difficult to refit. Lieutenant Stuart Chant's party were tasked with its destruction.

regardless, scrambling off *Campbeltown* only to arrive at the pumping station to find the entrance barred by a steel door. Borrowing a magnetic charge from Captain Bob Montgomery, who had been sent ashore by Copland to oversee the demolition operations, Chant, with trembling fingers, blew the door off and burst inside followed by three more of his team, their torch beams slicing through the pitch black interior. Leaving a struggling Sergeant Chamberlain to guard the entrance Chant grabbed Chamberlain's share of explosives and in increasing pain, zigzagged down the narrow, metal staircase to the impeller pumps forty feet below. Chant's dedicated band had rehearsed this scenario many times, blindfolded, in the almost identical surroundings of the pump house at King George V dock in Southampton and now their training kicked in. Systematically laying their specially prepared charges – 150lbs of explosive – they then pulled the pins on the igniters to set the fuzes burning. They had just 90 seconds to escape. The party, with Chant, by now limping badly, finally made it back up the stairs and out into the open to take cover behind a wall with just a few seconds to spare. When the explosion came – with a roar that, even though it occurred forty feet below ground, could not be muffled adequately and was even heard by Colonel Newman at his HQ – Chant's men saw great blocks of concrete fly through the air as the floor of the pumping house collapsed and the electrical control machinery plunged down onto a pile of debris. Afterwards, heavy charges were dropped into the conduits and culverts to complete the destruction of the pumping house before Chant – his mission spectacularly accomplished - turned to make for Newman's HQ.

Further detonations followed in the vicinity of the outer and inner caissons as the other Group 3 demolition parties from the *Campbeltown* went about their business to devastating effect.

The two winding wheels and electric motors situated in the winding house of the outer, southern caisson of the *Normandie* dock, the objective nearest the *Campbeltown* itself, was also thoroughly wrecked - at the second attempt - by Lieutenant Christopher Smalley and his four-man team. As the building exploded in spectacular fashion, debris was showered around the immediate area, narrowly missing Commander Ryder, also ashore by this time and standing near the caisson watching *Campbeltown* settling by the stern as countless gallons of seawater gushed in through her open seacocks.

His task complete, Smalley prepared to withdraw; first towards Roy's bridgehead and thence the Old Mole as planned. Passing close by Chant's team, there was a brief exchange of congratulations before Smalley headed for Bridge G. But tragedy stalked Smalley's success. On the way he spotted ML 262, under the command of Lieutenant Ted Burt, amid the chaos of the MLs near the Old Entrance. Burt had already landed - and by now picked up again - the Group 2 Commandos of Woodcock's and Morgan's teams. Short-circuiting his party's planned escape route, Smalley decided to seize the opportunity of disembarking on Burt's ML 262, rather than make for the Old Mole and risk missing a boat there. Burt, already under way, turned round to pick up Smalley's band. German ships almost immediately engaged the ML, as at last, it made for open water. Smalley, noticing the forward Oerlikon inoperative, moved up to man the terminally jammed weapon. As he wrestled to free it, in spite of advice to the contrary from the naval commander, it exploded, killing him instantly.

Chant and Smalley had not come face to face with Germans as they had gone about their grim business and had sustained no further casualties but the remaining Commandos who swarmed off the *Campbeltown* were not so fortunate. Skirting Smalley's winding house and Chant's pumping station, the demolition teams of Lieutenant Corran Purdon (objective – the winding house of the inner caisson), Lieutenant Gerard Brett (objective – the inner, northern caisson) and Lieutenant Robert Burtinshaw (objective – the outer, southern caisson but tasked to support Brett at the inner caisson due to Beattie's perfect placement of the *Campbeltown*), rounded the angle of the Forme Ecluse and ran a full 500 metres along its western

> They pulled the pins on the igniters to set the fuzes burning. They had just 90 seconds to escape.

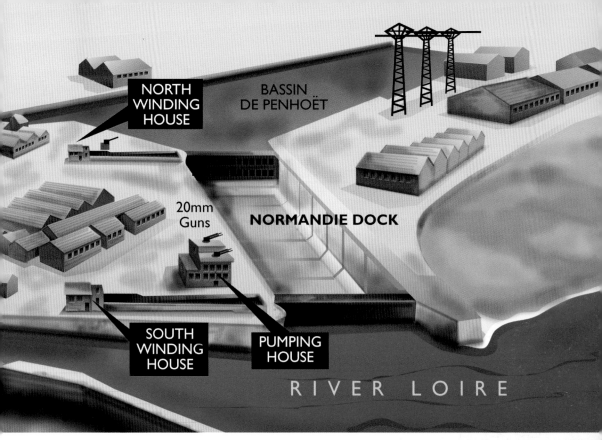

NORTH
WINDING
HOUSE

BASSIN
DE PENHOËT

20mm
Guns

NORMANDIE DOCK

SOUTH
WINDING
HOUSE

PUMPING
HOUSE

R I V E R   L O I R E

Three main targets of the **Campbeltown** *demolition teams. Knocking out the two winding houses plus the pump house, would render the Normandie dock inoperable for many months.*

Lieutenant Corran Purdon, 12 Commando.

side, following their reduced strength protection party under Lieutenant 'Bung' Denison.

Reaching the dock's northern end, Brett and Burtinshaw, laying explosive charges whilst exposed on top of the inner caisson, were lashed by 20mm gunfire and the firepower of six ships inside the dock, including two tankers laid up for repair in the dry dock itself. Their protection force, consisting of Denison's team only, was pitifully small. Assault parties from the MLs should have been operating in the area but had failed to land. Failing to prise open an inspection hatch that would have given them internal access to the caisson, they abandoned the plan to lay internal charges. Even so, the demolition squads still managed to plant their explosives and suspend twelve more 18lb charges from cords into the water on the northern, Penhoët face of the caisson, under a murderous fire. But the success in laying their charges at the northern caisson came at a price. Lieutenant Brett had been hit in both legs almost immediately and as

The twisted remnants of the northern winding hut blown by Lieutenant Purdon and his men.

German resistance became more organised, the volume of fire from the tanker nearest the caisson increased, whilst a small party launched a counter attack from the Commandos' rear. Lieutenant Burtinshaw was killed whilst storming one of the two German tankers inside the Normandie dock and silencing its occupants with Tommy gun and pistol fire. Six other men, including Sergeant George Ide, Corporal Blount, Lance Corporal Stokes also lost their lives.

Burtinshaw's RE sergeant, Frank Carr, took charge and blew the explosives on the inner caisson. Immediately, water swirled round and through the damaged gate into the dock.

Purdon's party meanwhile had smashed their way into the northern winding hut, laid their charges and waited for the survivors of Brett and Burtinshaw's parties to withdraw through them before detonating their own explosives to repeat Smalley's success at the opposite end. The obliteration of the northern winding hut was the final explosion of the Group 3 demolitions. The time was now just after 2.00 a.m. The dry dock would be useless for many weeks, if not months to come. The Group 3 *Campbeltown* Commandos had accomplished their set tasks in a little over half an hour but what of the other teams aboard the MLs?

Even as Copland's men had begun their descent from *Campbeltown*'s bows and into the maelstrom of fire which had enveloped her, the naval commanders of the surviving MLs had moved in to try and get their precious human cargo of assault, protection and demolition Commandos ashore. The *Sperrbrecher*, which had burst back into life a short time after the *Campbeltown* had rammed home, had added its venom to the increasing weight of fire being directed at the MLs carrying the Commandos of both Group 1 - the port column bound for the Old Mole and Group 2 – the starboard column scheduled to land in the Old Entrance. The wooden hulled motor launches, hitting back at the Germans with everything they had, endured an

Men of 5 Commando who were led by Lieutenant Burtinshaw. They fought a hard, last-ditch battle before being cut down.

horrific ordeal out on the river. They suffered grievously and the losses – of both men and MLs – were, in the event, too terrible to contemplate.

The absence of Captain Micky Burn's assault party 2d, due to land from ML 192 (Billie Stephens), and tasked with the destruction of two flak towers and securing the area in the vicinity of the inner caisson for the Group 3 teams of Brett, Purdon and Burtinshaw, has already been noted. In fact, ML 192 was hit four times in quick succession as she raced past the Old Mole, the explosions wrecking her steering gear and starting a fire that swiftly reduced her to a blazing wreck. Two Commandos, Burn himself and Lance Corporal Arthur Young, made landfall on the Old Mole after leaping for the

ML 192 was hit four times in quick succession as she raced past the Old Mole

steps as the blazing vessel careered wildly past them out of control. Three more Commandos swam ashore after Stephens gave the order to abandon ship. Even then Burn was the only one able to press on towards his objective, Bridge M, almost a mile distant beyond the inner caisson! He was the overall commander of all the Group 2 parties but now he was completely alone. Remarkably, Burn eventually worked his way to his objectives and climbed the unoccupied flak towers which he tried unsuccessfully to burn down before reasoning that he should wait until others arrived. Burn was later captured, along with Rifleman Paddy Bushe, while trying to fight his way out of St. Nazaire.

The story of the next boat in the starboard column ML 262 (Lieutenant Ted Burt) has already been recounted in relation to the saga surrounding the fate of Lieutenant Christopher Smalley's Group 3 *Campbeltown* demolition party. ML 262, damaged as she was, now made a run for the open sea and it was left to others to take the fight to the Germans. Unfortunately the same fate was to befall ML 267 (Lieutenant

Eric Beart). No sooner had some of RSM Alan Moss's HQ reserve jumped ashore than the ML came under intense fire. Baert immediately recalled the Commandos and, as so many had done already, the motor launch caught fire soon afterwards. Beart abandoned ship and machine-gun bullets raked the survivors as they thrashed about in the cold water - now covered with a dangerously flammable slick of oil and fuel - or struggled to stay on a Carley float. Moss was shot and killed in the water just after he had given up his place in the Carley float to one of his young charges, Private Diamond of 4 Troop, 2 Commando. Only three of Moss's Commando ssurvived to be fished out of the water and taken prisoner. Eleven of the ML crew, including Beart himself, perished.

Lieutenant Bill Tillie's ML 268, carrying two, five man demolition and protection teams under Lieutenants Harry Pennington and Morgan Jenkins, plus seven extra men earmarked for Newman's HQ reserve, was hit in the fuel tanks and exploded, killing half its crew and almost all the Commandos before it ever reached the landing point. Next in line was the torpedo-armed ML 156 (Lieutenant Leslie Fenton) carrying half the strength of Captain Hooper's twenty-eight man Special Task Party, ordered to destroy gun positions north and south of the Old Entrance. Already damaged during the run in, ML 156 now came under a murderous crossfire which first destroyed her steering and then caused her engines to fail. Although one engine was revived, with no means of directing it, the launch was, to all intents and purposes, operationally useless. It was clearly suicide to go on and the seriously wounded Fenton took the decision to withdraw in consultation with Hooper, also wounded. The launch was scuttled later.

Only three of Moss's Commandos survived to be fished out of the water and taken prisoner.

Up to this point not one of the starboard MLs had managed to breach the curtain of German defensive fire to effect a successful landing. It fell to the very last ML in the column to achieve this feat. Whether the MLs in front had drawn the German fire sufficiently to 'screen' Rodier's approach or simply that *Lady Luck* had sailed up the Loire with him, Rodier's launch, also torpedo armed and carrying the rest of Hooper's split force under Troop Sergeant Major George Haines, came in relatively unscathed and landed all thirteen Commandos. Rodier came in just before MGB 314 landed Newman's party and then, as was noted above, came alongside *Campbeltown* and took on some of her crew after Beattie had given the order to abandon her.

Amongst the men taken off were Lieutenant Commander Beattie himself, her First Lieutenant, Chief Engineer, Surgeon, and most notably perhaps, Lieutenant Nigel Tibbits, the brilliant young officer who had devised the means by which the destroyer had been turned into such a potent weapon of destruction and whose hands had been on the wheel when 'Campbeltown' struck the outer caisson.

Backing away from the destroyer's port quarter, Rodier's heavily laden launch picked up speed as she headed seaward. Tantalisingly close to safety, she was first bracketed by salvoes of heavy shells, then struck and stopped. Burning fiercely amidships, with petrol swilling about in the scuppers and with wounded everywhere, she eventually burned out while the few who survived the onslaught went over the side. Of the men taken off the 'Campbeltown' only a handful, including Beattie, survived to be plucked from the sea in the morning. Most of them, including the gallant and talented Lieutenant Tibbits, were lost forever.

Rodier's was to be the final landing. The starboard column had landed just fourteen commando out of a possible total of more than fifty, excluding those of Newman's HQ, and one of those, Captain Micky Burn, the overall Group 2 commander, was, as we have seen, working alone.

At the Old Mole, where the commanders of the port column MLs were attempting to land their Group 1 Commandos, the story was depressingly familiar.

As one of the lead boats in the column, ML 447 (Lieutenant Platt) came in for some gruelling punishment from the guns situated on and at the base of the Mole. Several men – soldiers and sailors - had already been killed during the run in and her Oerlikons had already been destroyed but as she made for the slipway of the Mole a large shell tore into the engine room setting the compartment ablaze. Platt abandoned the landing as ML 447 drifted along helplessly with the tide. Most of Captain David Birney's fourteen strong assault party of 2 Troop, 2 Commando were by now either dead or wounded and the assault capability of Group 1 had been effectively wiped out in one fell swoop. What's more the defences of the Mole remained intact. A terrifying prospect for the MLs which were destined to follow. As Platt battled to save his ship, Birney, along with Lieutenant Bill Clibborn and Troop Sergeant Major Hewitt, took their chances and plunged into the freezing water. So nearly rescued by Captain David Paton RAMC aboard ML 307 (Lieutenant Norman Wallis RANVR), Captain Birney later died of wounds and exhaustion, whilst his two comrades struggled ashore only to be taken prisoner. Just six of Birney's original party would survive the battle.

> **Platt abandoned the landing as ML 447 drifted along helplessly with the tide.**

Captain David Birney, 2 Troop, 2 Commando.

Following behind, amid a cacophony of noise now made more terrifying by the screams of men trapped aboard another launch burning furiously off to her starboard, came ML 457 (Lieutenant Tom Collier), carrying the demolition and protection parties of Captain Bill Pritchard, Lieutenant Philip Walton and Lieutenant 'Tiger' Watson. Theirs was to be the only successful landing at the Old Mole. They were just 15 out of the intended 89 to get ashore at this point.

Lacking the heavily armed assault troops to sweep ahead, and man-packing only a fraction of the explosives required to seal off the Old Town and protect the re-embarkation point, these fifteen nevertheless pressed on towards their targets. Watson's protection party was first ashore, quickly followed by Walton's with Pritchard's demolition control party bringing up the rear, after Watson had investigated the gun emplacement on top of the Mole, thrown in grenades and advanced inland, thinking it unoccupied.

When Captain Pritchard arrived with his demolition squad to blow the southern lock of the New Entrance to the Bassin de St. Nazaire submarine basin, he found that Walton's party — due to destroy Bridge D at its northern end — was nowhere to be found. Under intense German fire, Pritchard's men boarded two tugs moored by the southern lock and lowered their charges below the water line. The charges exploded with a roar, flooding the boiler rooms, after which Pritchard headed for the bridge which Walton was due to destroy. With Walton's party nowhere in sight, Pritchard placed more explosives under the bridge and then went searching for the missing lieutenant in the company of Corporal Maclagan. Pritchard was, according to Corporal Maclagan who witnessed the incident, killed by a German who rounded a corner at the same time as Pritchard and apparently bayoneted him just

'I took a couple of paces towards the German and emptied the remainder of my Tommy gun magazine into him'.

Second Lieutenant W.H. 'Tiger' Watson. 1 Troop, 2 Commando.

before being shot down in a welter of fire from Maclagan who *'took a couple of paces towards the German and emptied the remainder of my Tommy gun magazine into him'*. Pritchard's final words to the corporal, *'That you Mac? Get back and report to HQ'*, came in the form of a direct order.[5] The missing Lieutenant Walton's body was later discovered, together with those of his four men, all of them cut down by heavy German fire before they could reach their objective. Heavily outnumbered and outgunned, the survivors, including an ever-increasing toll of wounded, were squeezed northwards towards where they believed support might be found.

Lieutenant Norman Wallis's ML 307 carried the small demolition party of Captain Bill Bradley and six men of 3 Commando whose task was to destroy the central lock gate in the New Entrance to the Bassin de St. Nazaire. Also on board were Captain David Paton RAMC, whose planned aid post was the building at the base of the Mole on top of which was sited the menacing gun position number 62, and the journalist Ed Gilling. As Wallis brought his launch in she ran aground just past the steps at the tip of the Mole and was showered with a deluge of grenades from Germans whom Lieutenant Watson had mistakenly believed had made a run for it. The gun on top of Paton's intended aid post also joined in, adding to Wallis's misery. Fearing the worst Wallis withdrew without landing a soul and it was amidst the chaos and confusion as they were pulling out, that Captain Paton tried but failed to grab Captain Birney.

ML 443, under the temporary command of Lieutenant Horlock RNVR, sailed clean past the target and turned around but even though he engaged targets on the Mole and came by again with all guns blazing, his narrow window of opportunity had already closed. No Commandos would be landed from ML 443. Nor would any be landed from the two MLs next in line.

ML 306 (Lieutenant Ian Henderson) carried the demolition party of eight other ranks under Lieutenant Ronnie Swayne backed by Lieutenant Vanderwerve's protection party of four Commandos. Henderson's approach, fraught with difficulty as it was, was made all the more hazardous by the detritus of wreckage and burning launches which now littered his path. Henderson decided against a landing at the Mole and discussed an alternative landing towards the Old Entrance with Swayne, whose men were already forming up and itching to get ashore and get on with the job. It was clear to Henderson, however, that that option was just as difficult a proposition. In spite of the fact that his launch was as yet undamaged and thus still an effective fighting force and in spite of Swayne's protestations to explore further landing sites, he decided to abort the mission and make a dash for the open sea, much to the chagrin of the commando who, to put it mildly, were *'bloody annoyed about it.'* [6]

Thirty-three men were killed, including several survivors Wynn had earlier plucked from the water.

The last of the troop-carrying MLs was Lieutenant Dick Falconar's ML 446. Like Horlock before him, Falconar too overshot his landing point amidst the mayhem and confusion of the merciless battle on the river. Both of the Commando officers on board, Captain Hodgson and Lieutenant Oughtred, had been lost and, as in Horlock's case, the scenes of carnage being enacted around the Old Mole meant that a landing was completely out of the question.

The specially adapted Motor Torpedo Boat, MTB 74, commanded by Sub-Lieutenant 'Micky' Wynn, became another casualty. Relieved of its backup role of destroying the outer caisson with the success of *Campbeltown's* ramming, Ryder had ordered Wynn to fire his delayed action torpedoes at the lock gates of the Old Entrance, then take on some of *Campbeltown's* crew before setting a course for home. Making sure that 'Wynn's Weapons' had finally sunk to the bottom, her commander had turned about and shot off down the Loire estuary under a thunderous fire from the German coastal guns. Spotting a Carley float ahead, Wynn stopped to pick up two survivors and as he was stationary, three German shells crashed into his MTB. Thirty-three men were killed, including several survivors Wynn had earlier plucked from the water. Only Wynn, injured in the blast survived, along with two others.

The figures for Commandos landed at the Mole were almost exactly the same as those landed at the Old Entrance – 15 out of a possible 89. It was a pitifully small force then, which landed to add its weight to the *Campbeltown*'s Group 3 parties, but that weight, as willing as it was, was precious little to accomplish all the tasks intended. With the numerous casualties and failed landings amongst the ML borne Commando teams many key tasks of the Group 1 and Group 2 demolitions parties were never accomplished. In the sector of the Old Town designated as the Group 1 area, the failure of the parties to get ashore from the Old Mole and destroy the large lifting bridge and adjacent lock gates, the central lock gates and the swing bridge and lock gates at the seaward end of the New Entrance, meant that the primary crossing points, over which the Germans could launch counter attacks against the re-embarkation point at the Mole, remained intact. Even then the Mole was never wrested from German control, its continued occupation effectively dashing any hope of a planned withdrawal.

> ...the water's surface had ignited, casting a hellish glow on the charred and burning wrecks of several MLs and lighting up the still shapes of bodies...

The landings from the *Campbeltown* and the nightmare of attempted landings that characterised the river battle took place within the same time frame but Colonel Newman, who had established his HQ to the south of Bridge G where they were eventually reinforced by Haines' small party, was oblivious to the full extent of the disaster which had taken place on the river. A lack of effective communications robbed him of this vital intelligence and thus effective command and control proved non-existent. Although he had heard the reassuring thump of several detonations he nevertheless had to wait for news of the all-important demolitions in and around the dry dock. One by one the *Campbeltown* parties came in and as they made their way across the fire-swept bridge, passing through a small bridge-head held to the last by Captain Roy's assault team, few of the survivors had any idea that the failures at the other two landing sites had robbed them of their chance to make it home. Indeed when they joined up with Newman, Haines and the handful of men who had made it onto the Mole, hopes were still high that the MLs would be standing by to carry them to safety. Or so they thought. A dreadful and morale sapping sight greeted them when they reached the planned embarkation point as the effects of the full fury of the German guns upon the vulnerable Fairmile MLs was last witnessed at first hand. Outside the Old Entrance, the very Loire itself seemed ablaze as the oil/fuel mixture on the water's surface had ignited, casting a hellish glow on the charred and burning wrecks of several MLs and lighting up the still shapes of bodies floating broken and lifeless on the water. A maritime graveyard and charnel house combined. Stunned by the sight which greeted them, it was clear that escape by sea was now out of the question.

The same sight had temporarily stunned Commander Ryder now back on board MGB 314. Leaving the Old Entrance after Wynn, Ryder had been keen to see how events were developing at the Old Mole. The scene which had greeted him as Dunstan Curtis nosed MGB 314 into the estuary, had been so grim that Ryder was

ABLE SEAMAN
W. A. (BILL) SAVAGE

William Savage was awarded the Victoria Cross posthumously for his part in the St Nazaire raid. His citation reads:

For great gallantry, skill and devotion to duty as gunlayer of the pom-pom in a Motor Gun Boat in the St Nazaire Raid. Completely exposed, and under heavy fire, he engaged positions ashore with cool and steady accuracy. On the way out of the harbour he kept up the same vigorous and accurate fire against the attacking ships, until he was killed at his gun.

reported to have uttered, *'Good Lord! What the hell do we do now?'* Regaining his composure swiftly he ordered MGB 314 to act in support of the MLs at the Mole and Able Seaman Savage - assisted by Able Seaman Smith - completely exposed at his forward pom-pom and under fire from every direction, added further to his record of gallantry as he engaged and fought a duel with the gun on top of the Mole itself. Savage was destined to die in a final duel with a German patrol boat at around 3.20 a.m. as MGB 314 made its way back down the Loire on its way to rendezvous with the escorting destroyers. For his courageous and selfless service in support of his comrades in manning the forward gun that night to such effect, Bill Savage earned a posthumous Victoria Cross.

For the Commandos ashore their only hope of freedom now rested entirely on their ability to battle their way out of the ever tightening German noose. With the MLs gone, there was simply no alternative. They would have to fight their way out.

'OUR HANDS WERE TORN APART'

An Aborted Landing at the Mole
By Dr. David Paton - ex-Captain RAMC & No.2
Commando, Aboard ML 307

We approached the east side of the Mole but as we pulled up beside it we crunched into something submerged. Meantime it was all too obvious that the Huns were still on the Mole. We pushed our ladders up against the Mole but anyone who tried to climb up fell off, for the ladders were pushed out from above. Now bombs began to be rolled over on to our decks and we were all dancing about kicking them into the water. I turned round to see what was going on behind and saw a Captain of the Inniskillin Fusiliers falling off someone's shoulders. He had been trying to get a Bren gun up to fire over the angle of the Mole by standing on someone's shoulders. He assured me that he had killed a man but the recoil had made him fall to the deck. Meantime the skipper judged that we were not going to manage there and reversed out and tried to get along the other side of the Mole, but the boat ahead of us was now burning fiercely, all lit up like a film river boat. As he hesitated there, I saw a German soldier climb up to the Bofors type gun on what was supposed to be my medical post and load that gun with a clip of four large shells. He was alone but he managed to direct the gun by using two lots of wheels, one for aim and the other for elevation. Then I noticed my Red Cross armband shining white and fluorescent in the searchlights, so I took it off and stuffed it in my blouse. Then [the German] gunner fired his clip - he was only about 25 yards away. The first shot fell into the water only ten yards away; the next - five yards away. I didn't know then what happened to the third but the fourth produced a draught as it shot by me and splashed into the water only ten yards on the seaward side of our boat.

A shout came from the water just alongside and I was able to yank a British soldier aboard. He was distressingly short of breath for his Mae West had tightened up in the water and was compressing his chest. I tried to cut its ties with my dagger, but to no avail: then I remembered that I had a pair of scissors for just such a purpose and these gave him instant relief. Then another voice called from the water, which was now licking with flames. It was Captain Birney, a very dear friend. We managed to lock our hands but then the boat's propellers gave a great surge in reverse and our hands were torn apart because of the oily water.

Now my medical sergeant came up to me and said, "Do you know, sir, we have wounded below." I lost my cool and said that we shouldn't be worrying about that but should be on land and in that blockhouse which was firing at us. I looked to see what the skipper was doing but he seemed to be busy enough so I went below to deal with the wounded there. Happily the lights still worked and I was able to check that none needed immediate care. As I had dressed my first casualty I was rising to go to the next when the boat gave a great lurch and I was thrown off balance, kicking the poor casualty on the head. When I was free of wounded I looked out of a hole in the side of the ship to see what was happening and saw we were moving fast and in a zig-zag fashion, downriver in clouds of smoke. The Skipper had spotted not so bright areas on either side of the searchlights and by travelling in these we were not being hit anymore. By the time I got back on deck we had left the harbour and were racing for the open sea. I could tell the Skipper that we had eight casualties, none all that serious, and no dead. We continued grimly with our run for the open sea. Now another ML joined us, and together we made for the centre of the Atlantic.

St. Nazaire Operation Chariot - An Unpublished Account by Dr. David Paton (2002)

'BURNING MLS EVERYWHERE - A TERRIBLE SIGHT'

By Sir Ronald Swayne MC Ex - Lieutenant, Herefordshire Regiment, 9 and 11 Independent Companies, No. 1 Special Service Battalion and finally No. 1 Commando

We went up the northern channel in the Loire, which was well away from the coastal batteries on the southern shore. And nothing happened at all until we were quite close in, when the shooting started. We were one of the last MLs in the column so we saw it all developing in front of us. Not that you could see anything obviously at night but you could see the tracer. It was a very wonderful firework display. There was a lightship which we all pasted with the Bren guns as we went by. I think it was rather pointless. We gradually came up level with the Old Mole which by that time was a terrible sight because not only had the air raid been called off so that the [German] anti-aircraft guns could be used to shoot up the MLs coming in but on the Old Mole was a sort of emplacement. And the German soldiers in there found it very easy to bomb and shoot up the MLs as they came into the Mole. There were a lot of burning MLs when we arrived. So we cruised around for quite a time. Ian Henderson, who was the Captain of my ML decided he couldn't go in, I think quite rightly. I don't think he could get into the Mole. I agreed with him on that. I did think though that he ought to have tried to go in higher up. He was very diffident to do this. He said he didn't know the lie of the shore there. I thought the place to go in would have been perhaps east of the Normandie Basin. He said he had no idea how the shore lay there [and that] we'd probably just go down and get

93

shot up. What he could have done, actually, I think, was to have gone into the Old Entrance but you could hardly blame him because the fire was very intense indeed and there were burning MLs everywhere.

And so he eventually turned the ship around and we left for home with a lot of grumbling from my soldiers. They felt they'd come all the way to there - we'd been busily engaged in shooting up the searchlights and so on. I used a Bren gun till it was red hot and changed the barrel and took all the skin off the inside of my hand. It was a frightfully inefficient thing to do because in our regular instruction as soldiers we were always taught not to handle the barrels when changing them except by this special handle. So I lost the skin on one hand. But it was very good target shooting and I think we did a certain amount of damage. But it was very sad. So Ian Henderson decided to turn for home and towards home we went.

Sir Ronald Swayne M.C., *The Commandos* IWM Sound Archive 10231/3 (1988)

[1] Robin Neillands, *The Raiders – The Army Commandos 1940-46* (London: Weidenfeld and Nicolson, 1989) pp.71-72

[2] Kenneth Macksey, *Commando Strike – The Story of Amphibious Raiding in World War II* (London: Leo Cooper, 1985) p.84

[3] Robin Neillands, *op.cit*. p. 72

[4] IWM Sound Archive 22671 (2002)

[5] James G. Dorrian, *op.cit*. p.188

[6] *Ibid*, p.157

[7] C. E. Lucas Phillips *op.cit*, p.193

THE BRIDGE
OF MEMORIES

L ike Commander Ryder, who had witnessed the grisly scene out on the Loire estuary before him, Lieutenant Colonel Newman's first recorded words on reaching the Old Mole, reflected his initial shock. Staring in disbelief at the carnage now arrayed in front of him, Newman exclaimed to Major Copland at his side, 'Good heavens, Bill! Surely those aren't ours!' But just as Ryder had overcome his initial shock to get on with the job and albeit reluctantly take the decision to withdraw, so Newman quickly recovered his equilibrium and, as his next sentence revealed - incredibly under the circumstances - his sense of humour. 'Well, Bill, there goes our transport!' [1]

There were now some hard decisions to be made. All hopes of escape by river lay burning or drifting out of control off the Old Mole or heading downstream towards the sea. Newman's force, now numbering just under 100 taking into account those who had already been killed and the departure of the ill-fated Lieutenant Christopher Smalley's party aboard ML 262, out of some 113 who had been landed successfully, was surrounded by water on three sides. Trapped in the area of the Old Town they were opposed by the survivors of the 280 German troops of the 703rd and 705th Naval Flak Battalions, bolstered by men of the 2nd and 4th Works Companies. Most of these had seeped into the area of the Old Town across Lieutenant Walton's objective, the bridge directly opposite the Old Mole across the Place de la Vieille Ville, from around 1.50 a.m. It was this metal framed lifting bridge, still intact and spanning the northern end of the lock of the New Entrance to the Bassin de St. Nazaire – Bridge D to Lieutenant Walton who died attempting to destroy it – which was to become known forever by those who later charged across it and survived as 'The Bridge of Memories'. Ironically, with Bridge B being so narrow as to render any attempt at a crossing tantamount to suicide, it was Bridge D that was to offer Newman and his Commandos their only hope of escape.[2]

With the Germans now probing south into a knot of warehouses and railway tracks north of the Place de la Vieille Ville, squeezing the remaining Commandos into the area of the Old Town, Newman attempted to gather his force and consolidate his position. Major Copland chose a loop in the railway network, 150 metres or so north of the Old Mole as a rallying point. With the survivors of the *Campbeltown* assault parties of 'The Laird', Captain Donald Roy and Lieutenant Johnny Roderick thrown out as protective screens, the dwindling band of Commandos, many armed only with pistols, took the Germans on in an urban, close-quarters infantry battle at night with the same tenacity that had characterised the entire enterprise so far. During a hurried conference with Copland the idea of surrendering was dismissed out of hand and thus, now resigned to fighting his way out, Newman set about planning the means of doing so.

Splitting his force into parties of twenty men, each under a group leader, he issued instructions that each party, having fought its way out of the dockyard across the lock separating the Bassin de St. Nazaire from the Avant Port, would fight through into the New Town and then break for the open country beyond. From there, each party was to break down still further, into pairs, each pair instructed to head for the Spanish border and then on to Gibraltar. It seems incredible now that such an order could be considered, still more incredible that it be given. Here they were, a few score men, relatively under – equipped, running low on ammunition and almost surrounded by Germans, now being told by their CO to make a break for it, first against a force which outnumbered and outgunned them and then, if successful, to traverse several hundred miles of German occupied or Vichy controlled France, with no money or civilian clothes for a destination a thousand miles away. As ridiculous as it might sound today, by 1942 there were men who had actually completed such an incredible journey and eventually made it back to Britain. In May 1940, after the British had evacuated 20 Guards Brigade from Boulogne, leaving a large number of the 2nd Battalion of the Welsh Guards behind, two young guardsmen - Arthur Boswell and Alf Logan – managed to reach Gibraltar towards the end of 1941 after eighteen months of hair raising adventures. If these men had made it then there was no reason to believe that the highly trained, resourceful and self-sufficient Commandos could not. Newman's decision was perhaps not surprising in view of the tremendous Commando *esprit de corps* shared by his men and their sheer bloody- minded determination to see a job through to the end. In the event, five Commandos – Corporals Douglas and Wheeler, Lance Corporals Howarth and Sims and Private Harding – made it to Spain and later rejoined their units to fight another day.

By 3.00 a.m. all was ready and with the more heavily armed assault and protection party Commandos of Captain Burn, the kilted Captain Donald Roy, Lieutenant Johnny Roderick and Lieutenant 'Tiger' Watson in the lead and the wounded supported by their comrades, Newman's force ventured north into a

> ## Each party was to break down still further, into pairs, each pair instructed to head for the Spanish border and then on to Gibraltar.

warren of sheds and warehouses. Fighting through these the intention was then to loop back south along the quay of the Bassin de St. Nazaire and thus avoid crossing the, open, fire-swept expanse of the Place de la Vieille Ville in order to reach Bridge D.

The Commandos braved a welter of small arms fire from a series of small but dangerous nests of Germans who had lodged themselves in the warehouses and sheds and from heavier weapons firing across the Bassin de St. Nazaire. Charging on, according to Lieutenant Stuart Chant, 'rather like a pack of rugger forwards', through streams of coloured tracer and the screaming whines of ricochets, their circuitous route finally brought them to within striking distance of Bridge D where they halted and took stock of the situation in the last of what little cover was available. [3] Many of the wounded, including the already limping Chant, shot again in the knee during the advance, and the young and enthusiastic Lieutenant 'Tiger' Watson had to be left behind. The remnants of Newman's force were now just 70 metres away from the near end of the bridge, less than a ten second sprint under normal circumstances. But the intervening ground was level, exposed and covered by almost every rifle and machine gun in the vicinity including those in a pillbox on the far side. The odds against success were indeed formidable.

There was a pause whilst Newman reconnoitred the featureless Place. His Commandos waited. When the order came – 'Away you go, lads!' - there were no waverers. The assembled throng broke cover as one and tore for the bridge - Captain Roy with Lieutenant Colonel Newman beside him in the vanguard - as a tornado of German fire broke around them. Lieutenant Corran Purdon, whose earlier demolition of the inner caisson winding hut had signalled the last of the Group 3 demolition successes, remembered the charge.

> **'A hail of enemy fire erupted as we crossed the bridge, projectiles slamming...into its girders, bullets whining and ricocheting off them and from the cobbles.'**

'We all went for it like long dogs. I recall Donald Roy sweeping along the middle of the road, erect in his kilt, the cheerful Colonel Charles Newman, and the confidence -inspiring Major Bill Copland, who was a rock to us all. Other outstanding fire eaters included Lieutenant Johnny Stutchbury, Troop Sergeant Major George Haines and Sergeant Challington. A hail of enemy fire erupted as we crossed the bridge, projectiles slamming...into its girders, bullets whining and ricocheting off them and from the cobbles. There was a roar of gunfire...of varying calibres and the percussion of 'potato masher' grenades as we neared the far end. One of the latter burst at my feet and the explosion, combined with my own forward velocity, lifted me clean off the ground, wounding me in the left leg and shoulder. I remember landing on the back of the sturdy Stanley Day, No.2 Commando's Adjutant. I could feel my left battledress trouser-leg wet with blood, but, beyond a sense of numbness, my leg still worked and I quickly forgot about it.' [4]

C. E. Lucas Phillips described the breakout over The Bridge of Memories as,

'...a manifestation of soldierly purpose and of the will and determination

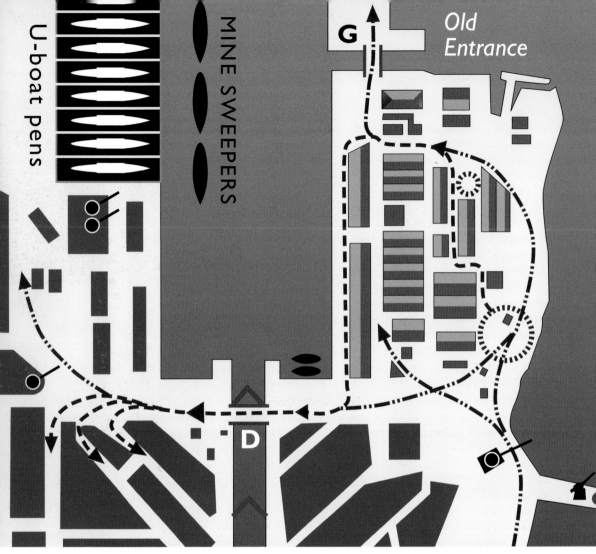

THE BREAKOUT OVER THE BRIDGE OF MEMORIES 3.00 - 4.00 AM.

Based on a map in C. E. Lucas-Phillips' The Greatest Raid of All.

---

to defy odds. If its purpose was not to defeat an...army, but to fight through it to the green fields beyond, it was nonetheless splendid in its indomitable spirit.' [5]

And the Commandos had spirit in spades. There is no doubt that an efficient and co-ordinated defence would have stopped the Commandos dead in their tracks at such a murderous bottleneck. Many accounts record that a great deal of the German fire was wild and high, men remembered the sights and sounds of the many bullets which struck the metal girders high above their heads. The inaccuracy of much of the German fire, however, in no way diminishes the depth of individual and collective courage which needed to be summoned to attempt the rush for the bridge That said, some of the German rounds struck home as men were hit and fell. The survivors pressed ever on at the double, reaching the far bank of the lock to smash through a German defensive line unnerved perhaps by the outrageous display of bravery from the men who overwhelmed them. But it couldn't go on. Advance units of the *Wehrmacht*'s 679th Infantry Brigade had arrived on the scene just minutes earlier and after a further 100 metres or so the Commandos were forced to swing left into a built up area to avoid an armoured car which had stationed itself at the road junction ahead, barring their route to safety. At this point the larger group began to

German soldiers open fire with a 20mm AA gun to flush out Commandos taking refuge in a building.

break down into smaller units as men sought hiding places in which to lie up and plan their next move. It was by now around 4.00 a.m. and the breakout attempt had lasted for about an hour. It would last no longer. With Germans swarming into the area, men forsook the streets for the greater security of alleys and back gardens, going through houses and clambering over walls and fences in what Major Copland later described as the 'St. Nazaire obstacle race'. Gradually they went to ground – in cellars, outhouses, drains and the even in the boiler rooms of ships in the dock - in pairs or small groups, whilst out on the streets the Germans rushed around frantically, blocking intersections in an attempt to seal off the area prior to organising a systematic house to house search. There were now just two hours left before sunrise.

Lieutenant Colonel Newman's party of sixteen took shelter in a cellar already converted into an air raid shelter with the addition of eighteen straw mattresses. Newman took advantage of the brief respite to assess the situation. Ammunition was short and the many wounded who had kept up so far were now weak from loss of blood. Some required urgent medical attention. Surveying the scene in the cellar, Newman was still keen to escape but if the worst came to the worst he was in no doubt about what he had to do for the sake of those under his command.

A group of very cautious Germans take cover behind a lorry borne Anti-Aircraft gun. This is part of a sequence including the photograph above.

German Kriegsberichter *film the body of a dead sergeant believed to be* George Ide.

> '*As far as possible, wounds were dressed and well-earned cigarettes were smoked. A watch was kept at the stairhead, and I decided that here we should stay till night - time, when we should set out in pairs for the open country. I also decided that if we were found in the cellar I would surrender, as the wounded were in a pretty bad way and a single hand grenade flung down the stairs would see the lot off.*' [6]

Any fleeting hopes of evasion were finally dashed when a German patrol crashed into the house above before dawn. True to his word Newman surrendered and the men were hustled across the road to be interrogated in what turned out to be the German HQ.

Little by little, in small groups, in pairs or singly, those who had crossed The Bridge of Memories - and those, including the naval personnel who had swum ashore from the tragic MLs, who had been left behind - began to be picked up as the German dragnet closed in. Captain Roy was caught in a police station which he had entered during a quest to find water for his wounded and thirsty comrades. 'Tiger' Watson and Lieutenant Gerard Brett were rounded up and taken to the Café Moderne where they were treated for their wounds.

Some of the men were captured twice. Physically by the Germans in the first instance and a second time on film as reporters and photographers of the German PK - *Propaganda Kompanien* - accompanying the German search parties at the sharp end of the action, began to record the capture of the Commandos in some detail as a propaganda coup. Captain Micky Burn and Rifleman Paddy Bushe were seized in their boiler room refuge of a ship in dock and were marched away, photographed as they went, into captivity. Others to be 'captured' for posterity included Corporal Bert Shipton and Lance Sergeant 'Dai' Davis and Lieutenant Stuart Chant who was taken prisoner along with a young Commando. Ordered to rise by the Germans who confronted them, the young soldier obeyed and Chant was horrified when he was shot out of hand. Chant's life was spared because by now he was so badly wounded that he could not stand unaided and the Germans saw that

Micky Burn (far right) and Paddy Bushe, being led away after their capture.

Above: A wary German approaches a shattered window holding a captured Thompson sub-machine-gun.

Right: Lieutenant Stuart Chant (seated facing camera), finds relief for his injured knees on the back of a flat bed truck.

*Probably one of the most
haunting images of the war.
Private Tom McCormack, suffers
in silence whilst nursing a serious
head wound which was to claim
his life two weeks later.*

he was an officer. Chant was also taken to the Café Moderne and later loaded on to a naval flat bed truck serving as a makeshift ambulance on which he joined other wounded, including the fatally injured Private Tom McCormack, destined to die in hospital a fortnight later from severe head wounds. It is a photograph of Private McCormack, sitting, slumped forward with his heavily bandaged head resting on his left forearm and apparently ignored by his captors, that has perhaps become, in its kilted tragedy, one of the most moving images of the Second World War. [7]

As dawn approached thousands of German troops poured into St. Nazaire as the local commanders grappled with the uncertainties and possible consequences engendered by the raid. All exits were blocked and the town was effectively sealed off from its hinterland. As the firing in the town gradually subsided German naval units took to the waters of the harbour, sweeping it and eventually bringing in the frozen, oil smeared survivors along with the bodies of the dead. They also noted with suspicion the spectral hulk of the *Campbeltown*, still jammed into the

*A frozen, oil coated survivor is
finally picked up.*

The body of a Commando sergeant, thought to be that of Robert Beveridge, lies near his intended target, the explosives still in place.

outer caisson. She would have to be investigated thoroughly in the event that she contained explosives.

Meanwhile the last pitched battle of Operation Chariot was, at that very moment, taking place forty-five miles out to sea as the crew and Commandos on board the escaping ML 306 struggled for their very survival against a far more powerful adversary.

'I'LL SEE YOU IN SPAIN.'

By Harold Roberts Ex – Lance Corporal, 2nd Battalion Liverpool Scottish and 5 Troop, No.2 Commando.

We were going further inland but we were carrying wounded with us. We moved across this bridge which was getting fired on. Instead of going on the top of the bridge I went underneath going from girder to girder, using my tin hat to get some purchase on the stanchions. Then I came across these big metal bollards and I was diving behind them to get out of the way. A shell burst against this concrete wall and shrapnel flew out. The chap I was with – Private Arthur Ashcroft - he got badly wounded there. He didn't have a tin hat, he'd lost it at the start and he had shrapnel in his head. You'd have given him no chance but he pulled through. I got spattered in the leg as well but I was able to walk. It could have been me. Arthur Ashcroft was lying there and I was lying next to him but he didn't have his tin hat. Another party withdrew through us and one of them gave Arthur Ashcroft a dose of morphine. He had like a little stud and he pressed it in. He put an 'M' for 'morphine' on Arthur's forehead.

You were nervous but you just carried on because you were linking up with people who were wounded and the group was getting bigger and bigger. We went into this house with this cellar to leave the wounded. By that time we were surrounded by Germans. We left Arthur Ashcroft and other badly wounded men in there. I met him later when we were rounded up.

The Germans were getting bolder and bolder and getting more troops up. We couldn't do anything, we had a lot of chaps injured, we just had to come out and give ourselves up. They didn't belt you or do anything like that. We just walked away. We were being rounded up and we were picking up survivors. We were herded into a hotel basement where we saw the Colonel and Major Copland and his party. The Colonel, said, "It looks as if it's ended now. I'll see you in Spain."

IWM Sound Archive 22671 (2002)

[1] C.E. Lucas-Phillips, *op.cit*. p. 214

[2] See Winston G. Ramsey, *op.cit*. p.14

[3] James G. Dorrian, *op.cit*. p. 226

[4] *Ibid*. pp. 228-9

[5] C.E. Lucas-Phillips, *op.cit*. p. 221

[6] James G. Dorrian, *op.cit*. p.231

[7] Winston G. Ramsey, *op.cit*. pp. 15-16. See also James G. Dorrian, *op. cit*. pp.255-6 and C.E. Lucas-Phillips, *op.cit*. p.227

THE FINAL BATTLE – ML 306

Lieutenant Henderson's ML 306 had pulled away from the area of the Old Mole at around 2.30 a.m. with twenty-eight men on board including very disgruntled men of the demolition and protection parties under Lieutenants Ronnie Swayne and John Vanderwerve drawn from Nos. 1 and 2 Commandos. The grousing, centred on the fact that the decision to withdraw had effectively robbed the commandos of the opportunity to do what they had been trained for, had rumbled on even as the ML had butted its way down the Loire and eventually out into the open sea. The boat and its crew had withdrawn relatively unscathed. Only Sub-Lieutenant Dark and Commando Sergeant Tom Durrant had been slightly wounded due to German fire whilst Lieutenant Swayne was nursing his own self inflicted wound, a nasty burn across the hand sustained when he had grabbed the red hot Bren barrel.

As the minutes ticked by and Henderson put more water between his ML and St. Nazaire, the men became resigned to the situation and then, naturally, began to look forward to getting home. They were well ahead of the three MLs - 307,160 and 443 - following closest to them and a dozen miles from the final group of three badly crippled MLs – 446, 156 and 270 – limping along in the company of Curtis's MGB 314 with Commander Ryder on board. These eight vessels were all that remained of the seventeen of Ryder's fleet that had sailed into the Loire with such high hopes several hours previously. Now they were all making for Point 'Y', twenty miles out and the first scheduled rendezvous point at which they could make contact with their destroyer escorts *Atherstone* and *Tynedale*.

Sometime around 5.30 a.m., with perhaps half an hour to go before first light, ML 306 was some forty-five miles from St. Nazaire and almost out of danger. Indeed she had already sailed past point 'Y' and was making a run for Point 'T', the next rendezvous point, a full ninety miles away from the oily, wreckage strewn waters lapping at the slipway of the Old Mole. But Lieutenant Henderson knew it was folly to assume that they were safe. Still out there, somewhere, were the five, 800-ton destroyers of *Korvettenkapitän* Schmidt's 5th Flotilla, sent out of St. Nazaire earlier in response to a reported 'sighting' and now heading home at a speed of 15 knots after a fruitless sweep of the Atlantic. Each of Schmidt's ships were armed with three, 4.1 inch guns in addition to machine-guns; still more than a match for a lone ML, its armament reduced to a single aft Oerlikon, twin mounted Lewis guns behind the bridge and the assorted Brens and Tommy guns of the commandos. Ominously, as Swayne's demolition teams had never had the opportunity to use them, the ML's mess decks were still heaped with rucksacks full of explosives.

Korvettenkapitän Friedrich Paul, Commander of the Jaguar.

Lieutenant Swayne was down below, with most of the rest of the commando contingent, trying to make sandwiches when Henderson summoned him on deck where Sergeants Durrant and Chappell were supervising the loading of ammunition into the Brens. Peering into the gloom ahead, they made out several dark shadows looming towards them. Henderson immediately ordered lights out and cut the engines to avoid detection but it was already too late. Two of Schmidt's destroyers, heading back to St. Nazaire on the reverse course as that adopted by Henderson, slipped past to port in the gloom but the diminutive speck of ML 306 had already been spotted on that vast expanse of water. On board the *Seeadler*, Schmidt ordered the *Jaguar* under the command of *Korvettenkapitän* Friedrich Paul to peel off and investigate. Time stood still for a moment, as the *Jaguar*, like its powerful, predatory namesake, reduced speed and circled round the MLs rear. Determined to make a fight of it Henderson's crew took action stations and the Commandos manned their weapons as they braced themselves for battle. Then, with a blinding, white intensity, the *Jaguar* threw its light onto the ML and fixed her in its beam. Henderson made a move and *Korvettenkapitän* Paul opened fire, his machine-guns tearing into the wooden-hulled Fairmile and the flesh, muscle and bone of the men above and below decks as he manoeuvred his vessel onto a collision course, his intention being to ram the ML and finish her off. In a display of deft seamanship Henderson managed to coax his launch round just in time to avoid a shattering collision and the *Jaguar* only caught her a glancing blow. Nevertheless the impact still pitched several men into the water, including Lieutenant Vanderwerve who was never seen again. Now the tiny ML replied with the venom of a disturbed viper as every gun that could be fired was brought to bear on the *Jaguar* at point blank range. The German ship now directed its heavy machine-guns onto the defiant ML, as a close-quarters battle of ferocious intensity developed, swelling the ranks of British dead and wounded by the minute. Sergeant Tom Durrant, replacing the wounded Able Seaman Alder, slipped into the harness of the twin, anti-aircraft Lewis guns and rattled away, automaton-like in his deliberation, at the *Jaguar*, despite being wounded twice more.

At this point, and having exacted a toll of some twenty British dead, dying and wounded, Paul moved off in order to allow his main armament to depress sufficiently to fire on ML 306, which it did to devastating effect, rendering Henderson's second in command, Sub-Lieutenant Dark unconscious, wounding Sub-Lieutenant Landy and mortally wounding Henderson himself. With the ML now a scene of utter carnage, both above and below decks, Paul offered an opportunity to cease fire and surrender. Lieutenant Swayne was by now the only officer left standing and he watched on as the *Jaguar* came in while Durrant called out for more ammunition. As Paul closed on the apparently helpless ML he received his reply – a long burst from Durrant's Lewis guns which ripped across the chart table in the *Jaguar*'s wheelhouse narrowly missing Paul himself. The Germans responded in kind and when a second surrender demand was greeted in the same way by Durrant, the *Jaguar*'s gunners simply increased the volume of fire until the defiant Commando sergeant was wounded so grievously, that he finally slumped, dying, at his post.

Swayne, only lightly wounded with several splinters in his legs, stood tall on the deck and, surveying the scene around him, almost apologetically uttered the words, '*I'm afraid we can't go on*', first in English and then in French, which finally put an end to the bloodshed. With a silence that must have almost deafened the survivors as it spread across the grey wastes like rolling thunder, the firing finally ceased. The final battle of ML 306 had lasted for perhaps forty to forty-five minutes. [1]

All that remained was to transfer the wounded and the dying onto the *Jaguar*, where they were treated in exemplary fashion, and search the surrounding water for survivors before hitching up ML 306 to be taken back into St. Nazaire as booty. Lieutenant Ian Henderson's and Sergeant Tom Durrant's lives ebbed away during that return journey, but Durrant in particular had, by his actions, already secured his place in history. A week later, an officer from the *Jaguar* recounted the story of ML 306's dogged stand and Durrant's contribution in particular, to Lieutenant Colonel Newman when he visited him in a POW camp at Rennes. Newman noted what the officer relayed and Sergeant Thomas Durrant – wounded no less than twenty five times - was awarded a posthumous Victoria Cross on 15th June 1945, the first ever awarded to a soldier for a naval action on the initial recommendation of an enemy officer. [2]

SERGEANT T. F. (TOMMY) DURRANT
I COMMANDO

Sergeant Durrant recieved a posthumous Victoria Cross for his part in putting up a fierce defence against the German destroyer the *Jaguar*.

His citation reads:

On 27th March 1942 at St Nazaire, France, Sergeant Durrant was in charge of a Lewis gun on HM Motor Launch 306 which came under heavy fire during the raid. Although he had no protection and was wounded in several places he continued firing until the launch was boarded and those who were still alive were taken prisoner. He died of his wounds.

Back to St. Nazaire. The survivors from ML 306 return after their capture to be photographed by German reporters. Lieutenant Ronnie Swayne (front right smoking cigarette) and Ralph Batteson assist Corporal Glyn Salisbury.

It was broad daylight when, at last, the survivors of ML 306 berthed at St. Nazaire. And just as German reporters and cameramen had busied themselves in photographing the captured, the dead and the dying when the final shots of the breakout battle had subsided, so they could not now resist the propaganda value inherent in *Jaguar*'s victorious return as they waited for the captured British sailors and commandos to come ashore from the picket boat sent out to fetch them. But while their view of her was obscured from the quay near the southern lock of the Avant Port at which the *Jaguar* had berthed, some 450 metres away lay the brooding hulk of the *Campbeltown*, still smouldering and still nursing her dreadful secret.

A cold Corporal Evans (right) and Private Bishop, head wounds dressed, offer words of comfort to Sergeant Chappell who lays wounded on a stretcher. Looking on is Private Eckmann (leaning on elbow).

Whilst the Germans celebrated what they thought was a victory, the smouldering hulk of the Campbeltown, *lay embedded in her target. The German circled on deck is standing directly above her massive explosive charge.*

'HE WENT ON SHOOTING UNTIL HE ABSOLUTELY DROPPED ON THE FLOOR' SERGEANT TOM DURRANT V.C.

By Sir Ronald Swayne MC Ex - Lieutenant, Herefordshire Regiment, 9 and 11 Independent Companies, No. 1 Special Service Battalion and finally No. 1 Commando

I was cutting up sandwiches below for the soldiers. The No. 1 of the boat, [Philip Dark] came along and told me to come on the bridge and to keep dead quiet and to shut up the soldiers. I did this and Henderson just handed me the night glasses and there were the outlines of three destroyers. I was munching a sandwich and it turned to dust in my mouth. It was a very funny feeling that because I didn't actually feel fear. It was a purely physical reaction. I suppose I was frightened but it didn't come into my brain, so to speak. It was very strange. And I had to spit the sandwich out.

I then went down and brought the soldiers up quietly and they all took up positions on the ML. The destroyer came right up to us and shone a searchlight on us and told us to surrender. We didn't and replied with fire. It was rather hopeless really because they were very much higher than us. However, we gave it a few bursts of the Oerlikon and the Bren guns and Tommy guns and they shot us up pretty badly. Very early on, Ian Henderson was hit in the head badly and his No. 1 was knocked down. He was hit in the arm and leg I think but not terribly badly. But it gave him a sort of shock and he seemed to disappear for a moment. I think he was probably unconscious, I don't know. The other naval officer [Sub-Lieutenant Landy] was hit quite badly and a lot of the soldiers on

Example of a twin Lewis gun aboard a Motor Gun Boat. They were fitted for Anti-Aircraft purposes.

deck were killed or wounded. Then it came in and tried to ram us - or it did ram us - gave us a glancing blow because we took a sheer across but it didn't actually do an awful lot of damage to the ML and then the destroyer went off a little bit.

I went down below to see what was happening and I saw holes appearing in the sides of the ship simultaneously, a hole there and a hole there. And one or two of my soldiers were dead down below. Then I went on deck again and the destroyer was still shooting at us and Tom Durrant, all this time, had been on the twin Lewis. Nobody understood Lewis guns in the Second World War but of course the regular soldiers were trained on them in the 1930s and he knew all about those guns. He was rather glad, I think, to get on this twin Lewis and he'd been shooting away at the destroyers regardless of anything that was shouted at him by the Germans. I started parleying with them and I think it was at that point that Durrant gave the Germans another burst at the bridge. And they really let him have it. But he went on shooting until he absolutely dropped on the floor, terribly badly wounded. However, I parleyed with them and there was no point in going on and I threw in with the ship. And that was all there was to it. I don't know how long it took really. It seemed an awful long time at the time. I talked to Fritz Paul, the Captain of the destroyer who became a personal friend and he says it was much quicker than I estimated and I think he would be right because I daresay somebody was logging it on the bridge.

We managed to shoot up the bridge a bit. His light was put out and somebody was wounded there. He wouldn't tell me at the time how many casualties he'd had but there were certainly quite a few of the crew of the destroyer who were wounded or killed because there were a lot about when we went on board. However, by this time it was daylight. We got everybody off - the dead and wounded. I only had a few splinters in my legs it was absolutely nothing. It was just like having been through a thorn bush and picked up some thorns. It was no worse than that. I was very lucky but a lot of the sailors and soldiers on board were either killed or wounded.

They took us on board and they were absolutely wonderful. The Germans really looked after the wounded beautifully. Philip Dark, the No. I who'd been a medical student for a bit, he was awfully good. He buckled to and he and I were helping bind up people. They ran out of bandages and they ripped up some of their linen to bind people up. We had one chap with a foot shot or lost a foot. I think he'd been overboard and he'd been picked out of the sea and I think he'd been hit by the screw of the destroyer. Durrant was enormously badly wounded, he was wounded all over and I nursed him for some time. Then we gave him some morphia.

I kept on getting requests from the Captain of the ship to go and see him.

I was very irritated and I sort of said, "F. off", you know. Eventually his No. I came along - previously it had been a sailor - and said to me in very good French that the captain really did want to have a word with me. I said, "I'm not going to be questioned by a captain" and he said, "No, he wants to give you a glass of brandy!" So I said, "Well, that's different. When I finish what I'm doing, I'll come along". I went along and I had a long chat to him. The treatment on the ship was charming.

Captain Paul was a very nice man and he later came to the prisoner of war camp which I was in, to enquire how we were getting on. We were at Spangenburg and he had some relations down there. After the war he became a friend and I went to stay with him. The shipping company, of which I was Chairman, ordered two extremely expensive ships costing forty million a piece from a shipyard in Germany, of which the managing director, a man called Dr. Hucksemeier, was [Paul's] No. I, although he wasn't on board the destroyer that night. He invited Fritz Paul up when I was launching one of my ships and then Paul took me off down to his house near Kassel, quite near where I'd been a prisoner. I gave him lunch in the castle where I'd been a prisoner

Sir Ronald Swayne M.C., *The Commandos* IWM Sound Archive 10231/3 (1988).

'NINETY MEN VERSUS TWENTY-EIGHT – WE GAVE THEM A GOOD FIGHT'

By Ralph Batteson. Ex-Ordinary Seaman RN Aft Gunner ML 306

Sergeant Durrant was a Royal Engineer before he joined the Commandos. I knew him long enough to know that he was a good chap to be with as regards being a good comrade. When we went training down to the Scilly Isles we had some rough weather and the sea spray was being blown down the barrel of my Oerlikon gun. Now on the Oerlikon you had a little cap to fit over the end to stop the spray going down the barrel. You could fire through it if you had to come into action quickly. My gun was getting wet and I couldn't find any covers. Tommy Durrant came up and said, "Here put this on". It was a condom. So I fitted it over the end quite easily but after it had been on a couple of hours, with the gun swinging up and down a bit, some of the water already in the barrel had come out into the condom and it was hanging down. Our First Lieutenant came by and said, "Batteson, what have you got there? Take it off, we're going to fight the Germans not seduce them." That was one of Tommy Durrant's ideas. He was always out for a lark.

We travelled as far as we could during the night and it was still very early next morning and we were supposed to meet up with the *Tynedale* or the

Atherstone which were going to help us get away. We were still hanging about at this point waiting for one of the escorts and it was still dark, and while we were waiting we saw these outlines of destroyers and we didn't know if they were ours or theirs. The Skipper stopped engines and he said, "Everybody keep quiet, we don't know who these are." We thought they were all going past. At least three went by and they were just far enough away for us not to be seen – or so we thought. These three went away and then there was another one following up behind. We thought he was going to go past as well but just as he'd got more or less out of range he must have spotted something. He turned around and came back towards us, switched his searchlights on and opened fire straight away. Of course, we had a go back at him. As soon as we saw we were going to get fired on we weren't going to sit there and let him knock us out of the water without any effort. It woke us up to the fact that, after 36 hours or so, we were back in action again against the Germans. I opened fire. As the ship is coming towards you, tried to fire at the bridge where all the action was. It was no good trying to fire at the sides of the ship; an Oerlikon shell would do some damage but it wouldn't put a destroyer out of action. You had to hit some vital part.

As the German ship was getting close, someone shouted, "He's trying to ram us!". The Skipper gave orders for the wheel to be swung over and instead of hitting us full on amidships he just caught us a glancing blow and knocked so many of our crew overboard. I was still in the aft gun bandstand when it hit us. One of our stokers, Butcher was knocked overboard and so was Rees. We found out later that Rees had had his toes taken off either by the propeller of our boat or the German. I never saw him again after that day. We managed to get Butcher back on when the firing stopped.

In the meantime every gun that we'd got was firing back at them but with the severity of the fire from the German destroyer it was putting people out of action and there were people getting killed second by second, not minute by minute. The motor mechanic came dashing up out of the engine room to see what was going on and as soon as he got up on deck he was covered with machine-gun fire and although it didn't quite kill him he was very severely wounded. He died later on when the *Campbeltown* blew up. They were so close they were within shouting distance and if you're within shouting distance and you can fire at someone with a similar gun to the Oerlikon you knew you were in trouble.

With Garner's [forward] gun being out of action he was helping me with mine. Landy was also helping to reload the gun. We'd already filled as many used magazines as we could coming out of St. Nazaire, to get them replenished. Garner got hit and he went down but I didn't have chance to see what had happened. He just vanished out of sight. Quite a number of Commandos had been killed and one or two in our wheelhouse as well. Tommy Durrant had his own gun and when our man on the twin Lewis got knocked out of action and fell away from it, Tommy Durrant shouted for some of the lads to get some more magazines and come and load him up on the Lewis. He was having a right go at them all the time. Then as things got more hectic and people were getting

Tommy Durrant's last sighting of the enemy. German T-Boat, the Jaguar and her crew.

killed right, left and centre there were only odd guns working.

My gun got put out of action. I'd got my duffle coat on and this shell came and grazed my thumb and went up and through, under my armpit. It never even touched my body. My motor mechanic, Stoker Ritchie, whose action station was with me, could see I was glowing all over. If he hadn't helped me to drag the duffle coat off I'd have been burnt to death. Another shell came and knocked the magazine off the Oerlikon and smashed it to smithereens. There was no use trying to get it firing again so Adam Ritchie and me were sheltering behind the bandstand which had splinter proof mats tied around the sides. Things were getting blown apart all over and when there was a bit of a lull in the firing I put my hand up to my head – my tin hat had already been knocked off at St. Nazaire – and it came away with all this coarse, white stuff on it. I thought my hair had gone white with the shock of the action. After further examination I found out it was where shells had gone through the bandstand protection mats and thrown this material all over my head. But I survived and kept my black hair for a hell of a long time.

While Durrant was firing he was getting hit all the time and they were concentrating on him as the other guns were gradually getting knocked out. They could concentrate on Durrant because his was about the only gun that could fire. Eventually we had no more guns to fire back at them. Most of the Commandos were either dead or wounded and when [Captain Paul] thought we'd had enough he came over, and said, "surrender". I remember seeing Lieutenant Henderson when I went round to the wheelhouse during the action. He was just against the bridge and he'd had his leg blown off completely. He was almost dead then. Philip Dark had been knocked out, unconscious. He was laid down at the side of the Skipper and the Coxswain. [Leading Seaman] Sargent, was killed. There were dead and wounded all over the ship. Lieutenant Swayne took the decision to surrender. He said we couldn't go on.

They drew up alongside us and dropped rope ladders down and we were trying to get our wounded up and on to the *Jaguar*. I went round after I'd got off my gun and there was Sergeant Durrant, laid out at the foot of the gun and he was absolutely covered in blood and riddled with bullet holes. He was a bigger man than I was and I tried to pick him up but I just couldn't manage it. He was still conscious and he said, "Go and help some of the others, I'm finished anyway." He must have known he was going. It shows what a brave man he was when he told me go and help someone else. My trousers were saturated with blood and I had them for about six months in prison camp, still covered in dried blood.

After I'd given Sergeant Chappell a lift onto the destroyer I went down below. I knew all the Commandos' rucksacks with all the explosives were down there on the mess deck tables. It was utter chaos. Flour had been shot out of the galley and spread all over the mess deck area and it was mixed with the blood of a Commando who was lying down there. They could have blown us out of the water right at the start. It was ninety men versus twenty-eight. But we gave them a good fight.

IWM Sound Archive 22668 (2002)

[1] C.E. Lucas-Phillips, *op.cit*. p.242

[2] Robin Neillands. *op.cit*. p.74. See also C.E. Lucas-Phillips, p.244 and Winston G. Ramsey, p. 19

THE LEGACY

For the Germans, the arrival of the *Jaguar*, preparing to offer up its water borne prisoners, almost drew a line under the confused events of the previous night. Ten hours or so of destruction and mayhem and the most confused and desperate fighting on both sea and land, had been visited on them like some Biblical pestilence, testing their resources to the full. Now on the face of it at least, the worst of the emergency was over. As German search parties and patrols continued to comb out the warehouses, residential properties and outbuildings for Commandos who had gone to earth, so others could begin to plan the reconstruction of the substantial, but not irreparable, damage caused by the raid.

Having first stared with suspicion and then incredulity at the shattered remains of the old destroyer jammed into the outer caisson, her snarling bows peeled back and stern on the bottom, the Germans eventually plucked up enough courage to board her as the minutes ticked by. At first a small cohort of senior officers and technicians clambered up the ladders so helpfully left by the departing Group 3 commandos but, as the minutes turned into one hour, then two, then three, they began to crowd onto her, rummaging above and below decks; some of them undertaking a spot of 'souveniring' and pocketing for themselves a small reminder of the night the madcap

Two Commandos in buoyant mood, are escorted away during the round-up.

A kilted Commando surrenders his revolver and helmet to a group of cautious Germans.

Above: A team of German technicians search the Campbeltown *and pronounce her safe, little knowing they are standing above 10,000 lbs of primed ammonal.*

Right: Once the Campbeltown *was deemed safe, souvenir hunters prowled her smoking hull.*

British tried – and failed - to smash their way through such a mighty barrier using a warship as a weapon. The technicians found nothing. Thus having been declared safe, the real business of re-floating the *Campbeltown* and towing her away from the all-important southern caisson of the 'Normandie' dock could begin – although not immediately – after which it was not unreasonable to assume that dockyard operations might get back to business as usual.

Coming ashore at around 10.00 a.m., just as the survivors of ML 306's final battle were being readied for transfer ashore, Lieutenant Commander Beattie, 'bearded, blanketed and barefoot', was also setting foot on terra firma with other survivors from the doomed ML 177. Beattie glanced nervously over towards the southern caisson. Unlike the British survivors on board the *Jaguar* and Lieutenant Colonel Newman's party of captives being held in the New Town, Beattie could at least see the sacrificial destroyer clearly as she lay there still, prostrate across her altar. He had but the briefest of sightings, however, before he was hustled away and taken immediately for interrogation to an office somewhere in the docks complex.

So, the old girl hadn't gone up after all. Beattie was bitterly disappointed. No human being could have done more to coax his old ship into exactly the right position and he was painfully aware that many of *Campbeltown*'s crew and Commandos, had suffered grievously in the process. All the efforts of the brave and resourceful Lieutenant Nigel Tibbits, the man who had planned - almost single-handed - the elaborate details of the *Campbeltown*'s destruction, the man whose hands had been on her wheel at the moment of impact with the lock gates, the man who was now lost to his family and country, had come to nought. Tibbits had set the three, long delay 'pencil' fuzes at around 11.30 p.m. whilst at sea the previous evening and, given a planned delay of some eight hours, it was already getting on for three hours beyond the expected time of detonation. Even taking into account an accepted margin of error beyond the planned detonation time, the *Campbeltown* should have been blown to Kingdom Come by around 9.00 a.m., a full hour earlier, at the very latest.

Hoping now against hope, Lieutenant Colonel Newman and Major Bill Copland's party strained their ears for any sound that might, even at this late stage, signal the final fulfilment of their mission, while Beattie's interrogation got under way conducted by a 'pleasant mannered' English speaking, intelligence officer. It was around 10.35 a.m. The German had just begun to regale Beattie regarding the inability of the British to comprehend the sheer futility of what they were trying to achieve by launching so flimsy a weapon as a light destroyer directly at the *Normandie* dock gates, when, in one final, titanic effort, *Campbeltown* unleashed the full fury of her 10,000 lbs of ammonal, with an ear splitting crack that shattered the windows of the interrogation room. The entire dock area and beyond heaved and rocked; the very waters of the harbour appeared to part for a moment and almost every window in the immediate vicinity was smashed as the explosion sent thousands of pieces of deadly debris – some several metres in length – hurtling thorough the air. Above it all, marking the place of the *Campbeltown*'s last and greatest act, a huge, black cloud – as from a funeral pyre - roiled high into the air.

Aboard the destroyer at the time were - and estimates vary considerably in the absence of an officially compiled casualty list - anywhere between 150 - 400 Germans consisting of officers and men who had searched the destroyer earlier and had declared her 'safe' and even military 'sightseers' some of whom had dragged along their wives and sweethearts to marvel at the gall and folly of the British in attempting such an enterprise. The eruption scattered their dismembered bodies far and wide and a French dockyard worker, allowed back into work two days later, witnessed the gruesome spectacle of body parts being shovelled together and the ground being covered with sand. [1]

The explosion took place at half tide and the dock was empty of water, although the two tankers, *Passat* and *Schledstadt*, were undergoing repairs. A tidal wave of water surged in as the caisson first buckled under the impact of the blast and was then bent back almost through 90° against its inner, western wall by the force of the torrent. The after-half of *Campbeltown* — her forward half having been vapourised in the explosion — surged into the dock on the wave, was deposited halfway along it and sank whilst the two tankers were hurled against the dock walls like toy ships until the raging waters crashed against the inner caisson which held firm.

Shaken again into a state of confusion and panic by the extraordinary violence of

The aft half of the Campbeltown *submerged in the* Normandie *dock, her mission accomplished.*

the explosion, pandemonium reigned as the Germans began to fire at anything suspicious in and around the dock area and in certain quarters of the New Town. They remained tense and nervous long after *Campbeltown* had disappeared under the waters of a now full *Normandie* dock, a volatile state which had only just begun to subside when it was again exacerbated two days later by another explosion at around 4.00 p.m. on Monday 30th March, some fifty hours after the *Campbeltown* had gone up. This signalled the successful detonation of the first of 'Wynn's Weapons' - the delayed-action torpedoes from MTB 74 - against the outer pair of lock gates of the Old Entrance. This was followed an hour later by the successful detonation of the second torpedo. Even though they were badly strained, the lock gates of the Old Entrance, unlike the outer caisson of the *Normandie* dock, held fast and all hope of rendering St. Nazaire tidal, therefore impeding the movements of U-boats in and out of their haven, was never achieved.

The detonation of Wynn's torpedoes finally closed Operation Chariot's demolitions account and rendered the raid's primary objective brilliantly, if belatedly, achieved. The Germans reacted to this fresh 'assault' with a frenzy of wild firing at anything that looked remotely untoward in the sensitive docks area - including shooting at their own men and on unfortunate French workers and civilians, some of whom were killed – but gradually the realisation finally began to dawn as to why the British had expended so much effort and so many lives to batter their way into St. Nazaire.

And what a strategic blow the raiders had managed to land on the Germans. With the *Normandie* dock now out of action, the *Tirpitz*, or any other vessel of any size for that matter, would be denied their French Atlantic coast bolthole. The largest and most menacing of Germany's surface raiders, raiders that may have helped tip the balance of the Battle of the Atlantic in Germany's favour, were husbanded into German home waters. In the event the Germans never managed to bring the *Normandie* dock back into service before they were defeated in 1945 and the *Tirpitz*, never again took to the waters to give battle in earnest, save for menacing a convoy in the North Sea four months later. She was eventually hunted down and destroyed in her Norwegian fjord in 1944. Even the French were not able to use their own dry dock to augment their post war reconstruction efforts – it did not come back on stream until November 1947, when it received its first ship and was only fully completed in April 1948.[2]

Sequence showing the destruction of the Tirpitz. *Unable to make use of the* Normandie *dock at St. Nazaire, the* Tirpitz *was forced to take cover in a Norwegian fjord where she was hunted down and destroyed by the RAF.*

Hitler had already ordered an enquiry by the time Wynn's torpedoes had exploded but instead of seeking to learn lessons from the events of 28th March and developing a co-ordinated plan to ensure such a raid could not be repeated, Hitler's search for the reasons behind the failure to detect and then repel the raiders only served to deepen divisions in the German High Command. Furious at the fact that the British could land Commandos on such apparently strongly defended German occupied territory so many miles from the British mainland and wreak so much havoc, Hitler had, the following day, ordered no less a person than Field-Marshal Gerd von Rundstedt to investigate. Von Rundstedt acted with alacrity and visited St. Nazaire on 31st March. His conclusions, that the German defence had been conducted as well as could be expected under the circumstances and that no one person should shoulder the blame, were not what the Fuehrer wanted to hear. Someone, somewhere must have erred and they must be called to account. Three days after von Rundstedt had reported his conclusions, General Jodl visited him and instigated a further enquiry into the failure to repel the Charioteers, the outcome of which was to lead to an unsavoury spat between those at the very apex of power in both the Army and Navy and only served to compound the factionalism which bedevilled the High Command.

Field-Marshal Gerd von Rundstedt.

The physical success of the raid – not simply a pinprick, hit and run affair - had further psychological consequences. The Germans became obsessed with the idea that further raids of this magnitude would inevitably take place. This obsession grew not only out of the physical act of the strike itself but also from a brief act of resistance on the part of some of St. Nazaire's citizens who believed the attack was the overture to the allied invasion of western Europe. The result was that large numbers of German troops were assigned to the coastal defences of France, thus draining the already hard-pressed *Wehrmacht*, locked in a death struggle with the Russians in the Eastern theatre.

As for inhabitants of St. Nazaire, there was bitter disappointment that the invasion had not, after all, been the precursor to their liberation and any further hints of French resistance were crushed as an iron grip quickly enveloped the town. But the raid did much to bolster the flagging morale

General Jodl.

of a French nation that had spent almost two years brooding under the yoke of Nazi oppression and was in dire danger of becoming used to humiliation. The detonations that echoed around the dockyard of St. Nazaire that night in March and the explosion of the *Campbeltown* reverberated around the world and signalled to the whole of occupied Europe – and to a United States now at war but still to be tested in the field - that Britain was capable of planning and executing bold and large scale, strikes against the occupying forces. As French Prime Minister Ramadier put it in 1947, at a memorial service to the raiders held at St. Nazaire: '*You were the first to bring us hope*'. The carnage of Dieppe still lay in the future.

And what of the human cost? The casualty figures, and particularly those relating to fatal casualties, make for grim reading. Of the 611 commandos and sailors who took part in Chariot, 169 were killed – 64 commandos and 105 naval losses, some 28% of the total force – and 200, most of whom were wounded, were taken prisoner. Thus 60% of the total force were killed, wounded or taken prisoner. That left 242, a number which included Lieutenant Commander Ryder, who returned to British shores, including those aboard the only three vessels - MLs 160, 307 and 443 - of the Chariot Force which had sailed up the Loire, to make it back to Falmouth under their own steam. [3]

For the battle weary survivors of ML 306, who had witnessed the *Campbeltown*'s explosion from the decks of the *Jaguar*, emotions ran high as they were eventually loaded onto a barge for the short trip to the quayside. Buoyed up by what they had just heard and seen they were, nevertheless, completely exhausted. As Swayne, Dark, Landy, Batteson and the rest of the walking wounded were brought ashore and dumped on the ground, incredibly, and in spite of the *Campbeltown*'s eruption, the Germans had assigned cameramen to click away at them frantically, intent on intruding into the suffering of the wounded for their own propaganda purposes. After the immolation of the *Campbeltown* and the destruction of the *Normandie* dock, and with German naval losses later reported as 42 killed and 127 wounded on top of which an unknown number of anywhere between 150 and 400 who went up with the *Campbeltown*, they would need every scrap of propaganda they could lay their hands on.

The care of the survivors now passed into the hands of captors whose treatment of them fell well short of the high standards of the almost chivalric code that *Korvettenkapitän* Paul had established amongst those under his command aboard the *Jaguar*. Cold, hungry and bleeding, the men tried to chivvy each other along, helped each other up, shouldered their wounded comrades and together were packed onto lorries and driven into captivity near La Baule where they joined with the rest of the captive Charioteers. It was in a field at Escoublac near La Baule, on 1st April - the Wednesday following the raid - that the mortal remains of those killed in action, both British and German, were laid to rest with due ceremony in the presence of twenty British commandos and sailors under Lieutenant Hopwood. They lie there still.

For the rest, long years of captivity in a variety of navy and army P.O.W. camps beckoned, with some men earning the dubious distinction of a transfer to Colditz.

There can be no doubt that the entire operation had, at times, been touch and go

The burial of the dead of both sides took place with full military honours.

Acting Sub-Lieutenant Arkle, accepts a welcome drink from his captors after being brought ashore from ML 177.

but in its accomplishment, secured at such a heavy price, fortune had, at last, chosen to smile on the brave. And bravery there had been in abundance. Five Victoria Crosses were awarded of which two – those to Lieutenant Commander Beattie and Able Seaman Bill Savage - were granted, not only for their own valour, but also in recognition of the bravery of the *Campbeltown*'s company and others of coastal forces. Lieutenant Commander Ryder, in 1942, and Sergeant Thomas Durrant, and Lieutenant Colonel Charles Newman, both in 1945, were the other recipients. The five VCs lay at the head of a staggering list of some 136 medals, decorations or Mentions in Despatches, many of which, like those to Durrant and Savage, were awarded posthumously. These men, and the men whose actions that night were not recognised with a formal award, had done their duty and had irrevocably secured the primary objective called for in the plan, a plan for which so many Commandos and sailors had sacrificed their lives. The raid on St. Nazaire has been widely labelled as the greatest commando raid ever staged. That assessment holds true. That the Germans had already begun to question the use of the *Tirpitz* as a surface weapon against the Atlantic convoys, thus rendering the destruction of the *Normandie* dock less of a strategic prize than the British had thought, should not detract

Lieutenant Swayne (right) and Sub-Lieutenant Landy take comfort in tobacco after being brought ashore.

121

LIEUTENANT-COMMANDER STEPHEN HALDEN BEATTIE

Stephen Beattie, Commander recieved the VC for his part in skillfuly directing HMS *Campbeltown* into the caisson under heavy fire. His citation reads:

On 27th March 1942, in the attack on St. Nazaire, France, Lieutenant Commander Beattie was in command of HMS Campbeltown. Under intense fire directed on the bridge from a range of about 100 yards, and in the full blinding glare of many searchlights, the Lieutenant Commander steamed Campbeltown into the lock gates, as instructed, and beached and scuttled her in the correct position. The Victoria Cross was awarded not only in recognition of Lieutenant Commander Beattie's own valour, but also of the unnamed officers and men of the ship's company, many of whom did not survive.

from the raid's achievements. If, by some switching of priorities of which the British were unaware, the raid had actually done little to rob the Germans of vital material assets, the success of the raid must be seen in a broader context than simply what it did or did not achieve physically. Operation Chariot was not, as Mountbatten had once famously remarked to Newman, merely an, 'ordinary raid', it was far too important an enterprise for that. And its importance remained, in spite of German thinking with regard to the deployment of the *Tirpitz*. Mountbatten recognised, as some perhaps had not, that the raid embodied fundamental psychological as well as strategic imperatives. For Mountbatten, for a British public aching for news of a military success against Nazi Germany, when the full story was finally revealed and not least for the Charioteers themselves, it had been no less than, 'an operation of war.' [4]

LIEUTENANT-COLONEL AUGUSTUS CHARLES NEWMAN - 2 COMMANDO

Charles Newman was awarded the VC for his leadership and inspiration, he was one of the first to land and held off the enemy with his men until out of ammunition. His citation reads:

Lieutenant Colonel Newman was the officer in charge of the military force consisting of 44 officers and 224 other ranks. On the night of 27th/28th June 1942, he was one of the first ashore, leading his men, without regard for his own safety, in the attack on St. Nazaire, France. They had been detailed to land on occupied territory and destroy the dock installations of the German naval base there. His men were so inspired by his leadership that they fought valiantly and held off an enemy far superior in numbers, until the demolition crews had completed their tasks. Lieutenant Colonel Newman, and his men tried to fight their way, through the enemy, into the open countryside. However, they were finally overwhelmed and taken prisoner, but not until all their ammunition had been exhausted.

COMMANDER ROBERT EDWARD DUDLEY RYDER - ROYAL NAVY

Edward Ryder recieved his VC for leading the MGB and MLs into enemy fire and remaining until he had evacuated Commandos still stranded ashore. His citation reads:

Commander Ryder commanded a force of small unprotected ships during the attack on St. Nazaire, France, on 28th March 1942. He led HMS Campbeltown under intense fire from short-range weapons at point-blank range. The main object of beaching HMS Campbeltown had been accomplished, but Commander Ryder remained on the spot for one hour and 16 minutes, conducting operations during the evacuation of the Campbeltown's men, dealing with enemy strong points and close-range weapons, all the time being exposed to heavy fire. He didn't retire until the ship could be of no further use in the rescue of the commandos who were still ashore. It was almost a miracle that his motor gunboat, although full of dead and wounded, had survived and was able to withdraw through an intense barrage of close range fire.

'WE KNEW WE'D SUCCEEDED.'

By Sir Ronald Swayne MC Ex - Lieutenant, Herefordshire Regiment, 9 and 11 Independent Companies, No. 1 Special Service Battalion and finally No. 1 Commando

I went back to the wounded and then Captain Paul came to see me and just as he was talking to me - we'd come into port at that point and I think the ship must have been tied up - there was tremendous excitement and bells rang and an enormous explosion had taken place. This was the *Campbeltown* going up. We went running up together on deck to see what had happened and the *Campbeltown* was coming down as we arrived on deck and pieces were banging around all over the place. It was very exciting and of course we knew we'd succeeded then.

Eventually they got us all off the ship and it was all done with great courtesy and kindness. When we were going over the side on to the shore, Captain Paul drew the whole ship's company up to attention and saluted us. I didn't know what to say to thank him. I'd concealed my fighting knife on my person, I thought it might come in handy for picking locks or something. I decided the only thing I could do to thank him - he'd been so kind - was to hand in my fighting knife, which I did. He grinned and I think he said, "You ought to have given that up" or something. He kept it for me all the war. After the war, the Americans made him break it because the Germans weren't allowed weapons of that kind and when we made a documentary, [about the raid], he brought the fighting knife with him and he presented it to me in its broken condition. It was really rather kind of him. As soon as we got on shore it was very different, I mean, they were just rough, that's all. They didn't actually stick bayonets into anybody or anything like that but they were unsympathetic and rather pushed us around. But they were quite decent to the wounded, I think. I didn't see any brutality to the wounded. They rather used their rifle butts if we didn't hurry, sort of thing. They put us into lorries and we drove through St. Nazaire early in the morning and joined up with our friends at La Baule.

Sir Ronald Swayne M.C., *The Commandos* IWM Sound Archive 10231/3 (1988).

"THERE'S A SHIP YOU WON'T USE AGAIN IN THIS WAR"

By Ralph Batteson. Ex-Ordinary Seaman RN - Aft Gunner ML 306

We got back into St. Nazaire at some time around 9.30 – 10 o'clock in the morning. They took us quite close to the Old Mole but not actually on it and there was debris floating all over the place from some of the boats that had burnt out. The German destroyer crew were all lined up looking over to where the *Campbeltown* was and we were lowering our wounded down off the destroyer onto the picket boat that was going to take us ashore. We'd just got Petty Officer Bennett on and laid out on a stretcher with Arthur Shepherd and two or three of the wounded Commandos and a German leant over and had a look at the *Campbeltown* and shouted down to us, 'there's a ship you won't use again in this war'. As he said that, within minutes, it blew up and you've never heard such a bang in all your life! It blew the *Campbeltown* to pieces. The front end got blown off completely and it caused such a big wash of tide that it made our picket boat rock so violently that we thought we might go under. We looked up after the bang and there was still debris coming down for two or three minutes after. Everything was coming down – bodies, wood, concrete, smoke and dust – we were only a matter of 300 yards or so from the *Campbeltown*. When it had quietened down a bit I looked up and I was going to say, 'well that's a ship we didn't need to use again in this war', but there wasn't a soul in sight. One minute they were lined up – fifty or sixty people – and two minutes later there was nobody to be seen. Whether they'd all gone dashing back to get below out of the debris or to go back on duty ready for more action, I don't know. We could see it had blown everything apart in that area.

When they took us ashore they left us on the dockside under guard while we waited for the lorries coming to take us away. At that time in the morning the news [of the raid] had got out and as many cameramen as were available made their way to St. Nazaire. The commandos that had been rounded up were practically all off the streets before 10 o'clock and we were the main attraction then – a group of prisoners off one of the MLs. They made a big fuss of us. They followed us around until we got on the lorries. Dozens of photographs were taken by the Germans and of course they appeared in all the German magazines and were circulated all over the world actually. The crew of our boat were in quite a lot of them. There's one showing Lieutenant Swayne and me helping Corporal Glyn Salisbury and Sub-Lieutenant Landy and Philip Dark are on it as well. You can see the size of me compared with the other two. Tommy Durrant was bigger than Swayne – a hefty built chap - that's why I couldn't pick Tommy Durrant up when I came across him on the ML.

We were sat about and then they came and moved us onto these lorries. The wounded went off to a hospital and the others who were fit enough, or just slightly wounded, were put in other lorries and they shipped us out from St. Nazaire up to one of the main hotels in La Baule.

IWM Sound Archive 22668 (2002)

"DOCTOR. YOU HAVEN'T SHAVED!" THE RETURN TO FALMOUTH

By Dr. David Paton - ex-Captain RAMC & No.2 Commando, Aboard ML 307

It must now have been about 2 a.m. There was little moonlight but the phosphorescence was such that on deck I could read the 'hatches matches and dispatches' from the *Daily Telegraph*. But creeping up from behind came a shape, always following our course and its bow wave getting nearer and nearer. Before we opened fire on it, we found that it was another of our ships, a motor gunboat, and it too joined our little fleet of three ships out of the nineteen which had been there an hour ago.

On and on we went, due westwards and as the first greyness of dawn made itself felt, we saw ahead of us two major warships on the horizon at full tilt and all their guns firing. This is it, we all thought, and we threw overboard all maps and codebooks and paperwork while we waited for the shells to fall on us. I went below to tell my wounded that they mustn't put too much air in their Mae Wests or I couldn't get them through the hatch. Then I heard an English voice on a loud hailer asking where the rest of us were. I stuck my head up to see our two destroyers *Atherstone* and *Tynedale*. I was arranging to transfer my wounded when they just picked up speed and disappeared towards France and we were left alone in the Atlantic, with no maps and no charts.

Feeling neglected we agreed that we should now head North and try to find England. Little did we know but we had passed Finisterre by a bare twenty-five miles. From behind now came a Messerschmitt 109. He circled to have a good look and then began his dive to machine-gun us from behind. But we fired before he did and he just flipped over and dived into the sea on our starboard side without even a visible sign of a splash. We didn't try to pick him up.

Soon a huge, four-engine bomber appeared. He too circled us respectfully from a distance, climbed and began his bombing run from behind. Some of our chaps fired and it was only too obvious that he was too high for our poor armament. So he took his time and slowly we watched as his bomb doors opened and then the bomb began its descent. I watched it for a brief period and couldn't stand it, but the Skipper was watching it all the way down. All I felt was a thump from behind. He had missed and we surged on. The bomber then left us for his home. Probably

Survivors from MLs 156 and 446 at Seaton Barracks, Plymouth, 29th March 1942 photographed after their return from St. Nazaire.

he had just run out of bombs.

It must have been about 6 o'clock in the morning now and ahead of us was a convoy going up channel without any protection of Air Force or Navy. Our own or German? We couldn't make it out so we adopted an arrowhead formation and closed on it, guns at the ready. We approached the rearmost huge tanker as it steadily chugged up the Channel. At its stern a sailor was busy hanging out his underwear to dry in the breeze. We asked him where we were and he pointed due north and said he could see Falmouth from his point of vantage. So we steamed due north and soon we were entering Falmouth Bay, none of us with any fuel left. The many ships in harbour dressed their decks and blew their hooters in delight. So those of us who could still stand went on deck and dressed our battered ships too but then Boyle handed me a wireless message he had just received. Sadly I had to order all my chaps below and they didn't like that at all, but 'orders is orders'. By now my one wounded sailor had died. As we tied up in harbour, the Brigadier came down the steps in the harbour wall and shouted at me, "You, Captain! Where are your prisoners?" Only then did I notice that my Red Cross armband was still in my blouse, so I put it on again and referred him to another officer.

Soon a couple of ambulances drove down to receive us. The only medical person on land was a crisply starched and very officious VAD girl, who told me that the doctors would not be out of bed yet. It was about 9 a.m. Now we had been ordered not to shave so as to save water and I had about three days growth on. She took me to one side and said, " Doctor. You Haven't Shaved!"

We went by bus to Plymouth to see the rest of our chaps who had come home on the destroyers. Sitting in the mess at Plymouth, trying to get through to my wife in Catterick, the other surviving captain and myself got a breathless message to get on the phone at the guard room, and quick. A Mr. Winston Churchill was on the line. Sadly I had to surrender to the infantry officer who had a chat with the 'Great Man', who wanted to know what had gone wrong.

And then by train back to Ayr, where I marched my sorry little Commando of three officers and twenty-five men from the station back to our HQ for debriefing. The people of Ayr stood in the streets and the women wept as we marched. They remembered us as the rumbustuous 400 they had learned to live with for months. We all got a week's leave; the Navy got a month and more.

St. Nazaire Operation Chariot - An Unpublished Account by Dr. David Paton (2002)

[1] C.E. Lucas-Phillips, *op.cit*. p.257

[2] Winston G. Ramsey, *op.cit*. p.23

[3] C.E. Lucas-Phillips, *op.cit*. p.265

[4] Kenneth Macksey, *op.cit*. p.83

FURTHER READING

Stuart Chant-Sempill, *St. Nazaire Commando* (London: John Murray, 1985)

James G. Dorrian, *Storming St. Nazaire-The Dock Busting Raid of 1942* (Barnsley: Leo Cooper, 2001)

Simon Dunstan, *Commandos: Churchill's Hand of Steel* (London: Ian Allan, 2003)

C.E. Lucas Phillips, *The Greatest Raid of All* (London: Pan, 2000)

Kenneth Macksey, *Commando Strike – The Story of Amphibious Raiding in World War II* (London: Leo Cooper, 1985)

Robin Neillands, *The Raiders–The Army Commandos 1940-46* (London: Weidenfeld and Nicolson, 1989)

Winston G. Ramsey, The Raid on Saint Nazaire *After the Battle*, 59, (1988)

Robert Ryder, *The Attack on St. Nazaire* (London: John Murray, 1947)

WEBSITES:

www.stnazairesociety.org

www.jamesdorrian.co.uk

www.combinedops.com

www.royal-navy.mod.uk/static/content/content.php3?page=2915

INDEX